The Challenge of Single Adult Ministry

Douglas W. Johnson

D1304499

Judson Press ® Valley Forge

THE CHALLENGE OF SINGLE ADULT MINISTRY

Copyright © 1982
Judson Press, Valley Forge, Pa. 19481

Library of Congress Cataloging in Publication Data

Johnson, Douglas W., 1934-
  The challenge of single adult ministry.

  1. Church work with single people. I. Title.
BV639.S5J63   259   81-19293
ISBN 0-8170-0939-6   AACR2

The name JUDSON PRESS is registered as a trademark in the U.S. Patent Office.
Printed in the U.S.A. ✥

Preface

A quarter century ago as a pastor in Boston I was involved in an effective singles ministry. The church didn't start it as a specialized ministry and didn't think of it as one. It was a fun group. It took time, energy, and all the other requirements of singles ministry; but the time was willingly granted to me by the church members because they saw the need.

Through the research I have conducted for two denominations over the past three years it has become clear that a first requirement for a singles ministry is the pastor's recognition of the need for such a ministry. It has to be a high priority! Our singles ministry in Boston happened without a conscious decision in our parish—but it doesn't work like that in most situations. As this book shows, a singles ministry takes work, planning, and commitment.

I am pleased to share the feelings, insights, and learnings from the research and experience. Both my readers and I are indebted to those who granted interviews, shared documents, and took time from busy schedules to talk about their ministries. The blueprint for active and effective ministries is a result of their work; any errors of interpretation are my responsibility.

Douglas W. Johnson
Ridgewood, New Jersey

Contents

Introduction

A third of the adult population is single. Single people are in their twenties, forties, sixties, and all ages in between. They live alone, with parents, with another single adult of the same or opposite sex; some have children. They are never-married, divorced, separated, or widowed. They are trying to find their ways, live their lives, and make their marks on the world.

Singles are different from married people. They move more often, go away on weekends frequently, and their ideas about sex, life, and recreation are less traditional than those of their married peers. Yet singles need the church in the same ways that married people do. Their problems are just as emotionally and spiritually devastating. They face the same difficult decisions about jobs, partners, travel, money, and security. Life isn't easy for anyone, single or married.

The increase in the number of singles in the past few years has made many churches feel they have to get involved in a singles ministry. This isn't necessarily true! Every church doesn't need such a ministry. It has to be done well or not attempted.

Singles ministries take time to start and effort to keep going. Results have to be measured in the quality of life of ministry participants and not the quantity of new church members. The leader has to be charismatic, organized, and willing to do the detail work of planning and chairing meetings. Clergy counseling time can be drained by singles. The continuous recruitment and training of leaders may detract from other church programs.

This book is designed to describe what is involved in a singles ministry. It is based on research conducted for two denominations involving over sixty singles ministries. A survey of existing, strong ministries included interviews with about forty people in twenty-five ministries. Full evaluations were made of ministries in six congregations, including interviews (three interviews over two years) with twenty-four people in these six congregations. There were less intensive interviews with the leaders of thirty additional ministries; information was also collected through questionnaire-type forms.

This book is not a "how-to" for programming nor a step-by-step plan for developing a ministry. It is written to assist a minister, church board, or singles leader in determining what might make one's ministry with singles effective.

1

Beginning Considerations

"I never realized how the church excludes singles until I got a divorce a couple of years ago. There wasn't any group or place in the church for me after that."

"Our church is located in a suburban area. There are very few singles around for us to get excited about. We are a 'family church.' The singles who are here are already involved in the life of the church."

"Perhaps we do need something for young single adults. We had a program a couple of years ago. There were about 150 names on the mailing list for three or four churches that were working together. I don't know what, if anything, is being done now."

The words and numbers vary but the themes are the same. Churches, in general, are not aware of the need, are reluctant to focus on singles in a special ministry, or are hampered in pursuing ministries for single adults because of the mobility of leaders and the transiency of the participants.

"Mom never said it'd be easy!" How true of a singles ministry! It isn't easy. In fact, it can be one of the most frustrating, as well as one of the most rewarding, kinds of programs sponsored by churches. It also can be threatening, especially for family-oriented congregations that decide to sponsor single adult ministries for divorced persons. Yet, the number of singles in every community calls for each congregation to decide how best to minister to those in its midst and in its area.

Types of Single Adults

Singles are generally inconspicuous in a congregation. They are not easily identified in a crowd unless the group is composed of married people who are standing with their partners. Singles come in all ages over eighteen years of age, which is the generally agreed upon onset of adulthood. They are never-married, divorced, and widowed. Another category of singles, usually a transitional state between marriage and divorce or reconciliation, is the legally separated couple. These persons are generally not involved in a singles ministry until they make a decision for divorce or annulment of the marriage. Their number is quite small.

The following table gives an idea of what percentage of each group was made up of a particular type of single within the total population in 1979.[1] For example, 69 percent of the men twenty to twenty-four years old and 52 percent of the women of the same ages were single. These percentages may be greater or lesser within the area of the congregation.

		Ages						
		18 to 19	20 to 24	25 to 29	30 to 34	35 to 44	45 to 64	65 and Over
	Single (never-married)	95%	67%	30%	15%	8%	6%	5%
Male	Widowed	*	*	*	*	*	2	14
	Divorced	*	2	6	7	7	5	3
	Single (never-married)	83	49	20	10	6	5	6
Female	Widowed	*	*	1	1	2	13	52
	Divorced	1	3	9	10	10	7	3

*less than 1%

[1] Table 1, from *Marital Status and Living Arrangements,* Series P-20, no. 349, February, 1980, (Washington, D.C.: U.S. Census Service), p. 20.

The numbers change drastically once age thirty is reached. Only 15 percent of the men and 10 percent of the women thirty to thirty-four years of age were never-married in 1979 while 7 percent of the men and 11 percent of the women were "single again," i.e., divorced or widowed. From age thirty-five to age sixty-five nearly the same percent of men and women were never-married as were divorced in each age category. Among the women, five times as many were divorced as were widowed in the age group thirty-five to forty-four. This ratio changed to about two widowed for each one divorced in the category forty-five to sixty-four years of age.

In most congregations one or more persons from each singles category will be a leader or active participant in the church's established ministry. They may not see a need for a separate or specialized ministry to other singles. This attitude must be accepted even as further study is conducted.

Never-Married

The never-marrieds come in all age groups. Some individuals, for family or personal reasons, decide not to marry. They may have no desire to become married. A congregation ought to understand that the never-marrieds are of all ages although the largest number will be young adults up through the age of thirty.

Young singles tend to congregate in certain areas, usually apartment-type sections of communities. They congregate because of job opportunities, social life which appeals to them, and/or living accommodations which are within their incomes. Many singles find roommates who will share living expenses. In today's world, these roommates may be of the opposite or the same sex.

Not all singles congregate, however. While many young never-marrieds want to break ties with parents but live within commuting distance of their family, another group lives in the family home with the parents, even though these individuals are independent of most parental control. Such arrangements may be made because of economic necessity or because no other suitable housing is in the immediate area.

One statistic for the never-marrieds shows some of the dramatic changes in life patterns characteristic of the 1970s. In 1960, 16 percent of the twenty-four year old women were never married but by 1979 this percentage had increased to 33 percent with nearly all of the increase taking place during the 1970s.[2] This doubling of the percentage of singles was true for persons between twenty-three and twenty-six years of age, key career and life decision times.

Another statistic of import, age at first marriage, showed significant change during the past two decades. In 1960, the median age of first marriage for men was 22.8 years and for women it was 20.3 years. This meant half the men and women were younger and half were older than these average ages. In 1979, almost twenty years later, the median age for men's first marriage was 24.4 years and for women 22.1 years or nearly two years later for each group. No longer are women or men expecting to marry early. Experimentation in living arrangements, money for travel, and pressure to build a personal and career life before marriage are factors which are influencing people into later marriage.

The point of this run-through of statistics is the *degree* to which the world in which the church ministers has changed. While attention during the past few years has been directed to increases in the number of elderly in the population, these statistics are a reminder for the church to look at all groups if it is to note accurately changes in ministry opportunities. It is entirely possible that different population categories will be major concerns in the long-range view, but now and in the immediate future these data reveal a significant increase in never-marrieds among adults in the middle to late twenties. This phenomenon has not occurred since just before World War II, forty years ago!

Divorced

A second large group of single adults are the divorced. As shown in the table on page 10, between the ages of twenty-five and sixty-five years, 7 to 10 percent of the women and 5 to 7 percent of the men in each five-year age interval were divorced in 1979. This statistic, however, tells only a piece of the story. It can't give the human side which is related to conflicts over living arrangements, children, jobs, and money.

One part of a divorced couple may continue to live in the previous home for awhile. However, divorced persons, like all singles, must find living accommodations which are within their means. This usually requires relocation either to an apartment or to other less expensive housing.

[2] *Marital Status and Living Arrangements,* Series P-20, no. 349, February, 1980.

Of concern in singles ministries are the households headed by women, many with children. Since women traditionally have been unable to find jobs with salary parity to men and because many women have not had training or experience which qualifies them for higher paying jobs, households headed by divorced females tend to suffer economically from divorce more than those headed by men.

Another kind of divorced person is one whose marriage has terminated with no children being involved and both parties having adequate finances. The life-styles of new singles in this category are quite different from the life-styles of those who have children and little money. Mixing the two groups in a ministry is a difficult task for many leaders. Affluent people and those with a scarcity of finances are always hard to put together in one group.

These examples underscore the fact that the word "divorced" camouflages a complex of broken relationships. The state of being divorced is different for each person. It produces separation and pain for most, but it gives release and a new charter for life to others. A singles ministry planner needs to understand the different aspects of divorce if he or she is to provide meaningful programs.

Older divorced persons may have grown children whose sensitivities and feelings of propriety overshadow the decisions of the parents. These feelings continue to impinge on the hopes and aspirations of the separated couple.

On the other hand, some divorced persons have young children and teenagers. These young people affect the amount and kinds of activities in which the single-again parent is interested and/or can become involved. Money, time, and obligations to the children may limit the fulfillment of a single parent's desires in a way in which a childless single would not be limited.

Yet divorced persons with no children may have other complications related to older parents and/or other relatives. Most divorced persons have some family relationships which must be maintained and which exert pressures upon them.

While external forces of family and relatives are important differentiations among divorced persons, more subtle separating factors concern the varying levels of self-sufficiency in terms of income and of skills individuals bring to the single state. The financial cost of participation or the level of skills needed to lead a singles ministry may count some divorced persons out. Individuals may need to refurbish or acquire marketable skills and so may not have time for such a ministry. The ever-present problem of finding reliable baby-sitters may rule out the involvement of still others.

It is accurate but not sufficient to state that the number of divorced people has risen dramatically. Congregations must go a step beyond the statistical indicators to look at the type of divorced person who may be included or excluded by a ministry. While there are needs common to divorced people just as there are needs common to families, differences are real and must be addressed while planning the ministry.

Widowed

The third general group of single adults is the widowed. These persons constitute a small percentage of singles under thirty-five years of age but the group becomes quite large, especially among women, once the age of fifty years is reached. One reason for this increase is that most women marry older men or men of the same age; since women have a longer life span, they outlive their spouses.

Widowed persons in the congregation tend to be a part of its ongoing life. They tend to live where they previously resided, at least for awhile. As part of a couple, they established a network of friends and so find support from the church during their times of crisis. In some instances, as when members knew of the spouse's fatal illness, the death may have been preceded and followed by congregation-wide prayer and mutual support activities. Unless there is a major community crisis such as a tornado, earthquake, accident, flood, or the like, where many widows are created instantly, the widowed individual receives a different response from the congregation than does a person who divorces.

It is unlikely that a large number of widows will become involved in singles groups; widows tend to be older and have interests different from either the divorced or never-married. There are relatively few widows under fifty while the highest percentage of divorced persons are twenty-five to fifty years old. Family situations, careers, and support groups are quite different for the two groups.

Few widowed persons were participants in singles ministries which I contacted over the past three years. The one exception was in a community which had experienced a natural disaster. The singles group began because of instant widowhood among several members of a relatively large congregation.

A cautionary note needs to be sounded. Programs for senior citizens are not considered singles programs by most congregations although many single adults may be involved. Senior programs emphasize fellowship and social involvement in a variety of activities. Many divide along sex lines; others separate the very elderly from the more active seniors. The problems seniors face are quite different in degree from those confronted by younger singles.

If a congregation decides to develop a singles ministry and during its fact-finding discovers a large number of singles over fifty years, a special ministry might be developed for these persons. This would not be a singles ministry in the usual sense and would not preclude the need for a singles ministry for those under fifty years of age.

Why a Singles Ministry?

Statistical Indicators

One of the reasons for facing the decision to become involved in a singles ministry is found in statistics. Census publications show there are millions more singles today than a decade ago and, given the trends, more singles will be in the population during the next decade.

In 1979, approximately 17 million men and 13.6 million women over eighteen years of age were single.[3] This represented about 40 percent of the male and female population in the U.S. at the end of the 1970s.

Human Needs

While the statistics are impressive, an awareness of human needs may be more effective in persuading some congregations at least to look seriously at the possibility of a singles ministry. Conversations with participants and leaders of single adult ministries reveal a compulsion people have to seek out the church during the crises of divorce, death, and other life-changing events. People come searching for counsel, for a group within which they can share their feelings and find understanding and support. They come to learn how to face present and future decisions about their lives as singles.

"It is difficult if not impossible for someone who has not experienced

[3]*Marital Status and Living Arrangements,* Series P-20, no. 349, February, 1980.

it to understand the total revision of life after the divorce or death of a spouse. Feelings of loneliness, fright, inadequacy, and guilt are like a huge ball and chain suddenly placed on the psyche. You *need* people who can listen, be sympathetic, and support you during these deadly self-doubt times. You need people to *give,* not demand from you.''

These words seem to summarize best the emotions which grip a person who faces divorce or the death of a spouse. The ''single-again'' is trying to ''make it one day at a time,'' and the church should not turn itself away from this need. It must either provide a ministry which includes this person or direct the individual to an existing ministry.

Of course not all people who come to singles ministries are there as a result of a recent separation. Many singles have grown up in the church and choose to come to its activities. They are not to be overlooked when others with hurts and pain seek the fellowship and support of the church. Yet those with immediate need oftentimes are responsible for churches becoming interested in a singles ministry.

The types of singles identified earlier, i.e., never-married, divorced with younger children, divorced with no children, divorced with older children, and widowed, present a congregation with many different ministry opportunities. Each group may find a home in one church if that congregation is willing to do its homework well, extend its energy in assisting the group to find leaders and resources, and focus programs so they are useful and interesting to each kind of single.

Individual Support Needs

Yet, the purpose of a singles ministry is not understood only through statistics or an awareness of human need. Putting itself in the place of singles, each congregation must answer the question, ''What can a singles ministry do for me?'' Leaders of singles ministries have responded by citing the reasons singles gave for joining their ministries.

''I wanted an alternative to the singles bars.''

''My whole world collapsed when I got divorced. I needed a supportive group to help me through that time.''

''Becoming a widowed person is like starting all over but with a lot different perspective. I needed the continued relationships of the past but also something else—a place to go to help me cope as an individual.''

''My sheltered existence stopped with the divorce. I had to be a person. You don't become that by yourself. You need a non-threatening group who understands.''

According to these persons, their church-related singles group provided them with unique and essential support. From their point of view, a singles ministry is crucial.

"It is a place to go where people don't ask you for something.''

"It holds the hope for congeniality, support, low-cost fun, and friends.''

"It is a place to go to learn and talk with others like yourself. It helps you think.''

Spiritual Food

The singles whose comments are given found congregations which were interested in helping people discover a purpose and meaning in life no matter if they were single or married. The congregations understood the singles ministry as living out the gospel, the Good News of love, kindness, and support with God's people.

Jesus said, "Feed my sheep." This is an important message to heed no matter what the nature of the group. People come to the church seeking spiritual food. The church, in order to be true to itself, must provide the food.

The primary emphases of church-related singles programs seem to have changed during the past year from psychological self-help to spiritual nurture. Single people are searching for a purpose beyond themselves to which they can attach their lives. This is not a characteristic peculiar to the single; it is common to the culture. Helping to guide people in that search and showing them essential ingredients of life is the primary intent of the church.

Separate Singles Programs

Some people argue against the need for separate programs for singles by saying that such ministries would isolate or brand the participants as singles.

"We can't start a group in our church because the single people I know don't want to be known as singles. They prefer to be part of the regular church.''

"Our group was going for a while but some of the singles felt uncomfortable in being set aside in a special class. They felt like they were stigmatized or something with that class. We finally disbanded it and the singles who stayed have gone into other classes.''

"We were told before we started that singles wouldn't want to be identified as singles; they would not come, and our idea wouldn't work in this church. We're stubborn so we tried it. Our group on Sunday morning is divided into three classes of about thirty-five each and our evening sessions draw upwards of three hundred people. Somebody was reading the signals wrong.''

The first two quotes are from a minister and a married woman who were acting as coordinators of a singles ministry in their respective congregations. Neither of them was especially sensitive to the need for a singles ministry and both were convinced it would not be important to their congregations. Neither spoke for individuals who were currently not in the church or who were not involved in one of its organizations. It's little wonder these ministries didn't take root. With that kind of encouragement any potential group need have no other impediments. The third quote shows, however, that obstacles can be overcome.

A singles program which fails because singles do not want to be set apart is better than one which was never begun. The reason is simple: It is better to brand and separate groups *within* the church than it is to ignore them and drive them *from* or keep them *out* of the church.

An assumption within many congregations is that singles do not want to be identified as singles. This may be true of some, but most singles are not ashamed of the condition and feel little need to deny it. They prefer to handle their needs as singles in ways that are constructive.

For instance, they covet illustrations and experiences which deal with singles. This is the reason most of the classes which are for singles have kept going in spite of low levels of support from pastor and congregation and the feeling of some church leaders that singles don't want separate classes. There is a need for singles ministries regardless of what church leaders may think.

As noted before, widowed persons are less likely to want to be known as singles than are never-marrieds and divorced individuals. The circumstances surrounding widowhood are different from those in divorce, and the widowed person is more likely to be accepted quickly by a congregation. This is especially true of the widowed person who has been active in the congregation. The continuing ties are reinforced rather than severed.

This is not the case with divorced people. Many members in a congregation view a marital breakup as a failure. In a sense, each of the parties of the divorce becomes a threat to the married constituency of the congregation. In addition, the fact of divorce indicates the fragility of any marriage. Thus, something subconscious is at work in the relationship between divorced and married members in a congregation. It takes time and a lot of work on both sides before they can accept each other. In the meantime, the single person needs a supportive group which can assist her or him to work through feelings of pain, failure, and frustration.

Young adults probably will be targeted in a group established for them. Some churches put people in this age group (usually under thirty although some keep it for persons under twenty-five) together whether they are single or married. Many will have been a part of the youth group of the church and will feel no need to make a switch to a ministry specifically for singles. At about age twenty-five, however, the distinction between never-marrieds and young couples tends to become clearer. Several of the young couples will have become parents which changes their life-styles in subtle ways. At this point, the never-marrieds are more willing to be put together in a singles group. Never-marrieds over thirty-five will have made ties with other groups in the congregation and may not wish to join a singles ministry.

The descriptions of persons who might be less willing to be recognized as singles will vary with each congregation. However, the most resistant to the tag will be some widows, older never-marrieds, and a few persons who are divorced. Most singles will not mind the distinction and will not be disturbed by a group of their own. Many will be quite pleased at the thoughtfulness of the church for this additional program.

Just because a class or group is formed for singles does not mean all singles ought to be forced into it. Many women and men do not like to attend classes or gatherings designated for a specific group. On the other hand, the myth of opposition to forming a class because it will label people ought to be put to rest. Other kinds of groups are formed for special interests or needs, why not one for singles?

It is conceded in various research studies that a primary reason for one's coming to church is because one's friends attend. In fact, many church growth techniques are based on friends inviting friends. When a person is different, in this case single, and has no one to relate to, it makes coming to church a difficult experience. The same reasons also make dropping out of church easier. A singles group provides a place where such a person can fit in.

Two Final Considerations

All of the arguments stated so far give powerful reasons for sponsoring singles ministries. They address the purposes of the church which are to extend its message and to meet specific human needs. While other reasons are associated with having a singles ministry, such as providing opportunity for singles to volunteer and serve in the church, providing Christian education for children of divorced parents, helping older citizens find social companionship, and the like, two other supporting points need to be mentioned. In the first place, in a viable single adult group some of the singles will find partners. This is not by design; it just happens. Usually this takes place over time, and the new couples find easy entry into the broader life of the church because they have been involved in the singles ministry.

One note of caution: Single ministries are *not* dating groups or places to come to find a spouse. This is not the purpose of a good singles ministry. Providing a non-threatening and non-coercive atmosphere in which singles can learn, share, and gain strength are the proper goals of a singles ministry. If pairing off happens, so be it.

A second caution: One of the most difficult tasks of single adult ministry is maintaining an adequate male-female balance. In most ministries women outnumber the men. If this happens it may mean: (1) the current program ought to be revised to make it more enticing to men, (2) a "recruit the men" program may be needed, (3) the number of women is threatening to men, or (4) there may be no men in the area.

On the other hand, a predominance of one sex does not mean a singles ministry is deficient. The viability of a group is tested by how effectively it is meeting the needs of the people it attracts. The sex of these persons is immaterial. While it may be desirable in some settings to have an even balance of males and females, it is not necessary for a ministry to be effective.

Second, a singles ministry may result in an increase in church growth and vitality. An effective singles ministry will attract non-church members. These people come for personal reasons and, if they find the group supportive and the program attractive, they may stay and find a church home. Numerous examples could be cited of people who got involved in a singles program and gradually became a part of the official life of the church.

Singles do not necessarily become married; some never do. A ministry should not press toward or away from marriage. But a singles ministry makes it more possible for people to come into the church and give themselves through it to a larger ministry.

A Conscious Decision

The decision of a church to become involved with singles in a ministry may be based on an assessment of singles' special needs, an awareness of their number because so many are in the congregation, or research on the number of singles and existing ministries for them in the community. A decision about a singles ministry need not be complicated, but a congregation cannot let itself slide into a singles ministry. If a half-hearted effort at planning for one is made, a singles ministry will fail.

Perhaps the outstanding difference between a singles ministry and other ministries of a congregation is the general lack of compulsion for singles to become involved. When families are the focus of a ministry, one family member often may be convinced of the attractiveness of the program and help get other family members involved. Children and youth are often participants in the church because of parental influence. Single adults are just that—for them, participation is a *personal* decision. In fact, each single person must be convinced of the ministry's ability to meet her or his needs. No one is going to force a single adult to attend.

In a single adult ministry, the program must be broad enough and the group attractive enough to convince singles to come once and then return for more. This is one reason a conscious decision by a congregation to get involved is critical. A congregation which thinks it ought to tinker around and experiment will not succeed. Single adults are looking for substance. On the other hand, a congregation which tries to control all aspects of a ministry in the same way it controls youth and early adolescent ministries is in for a rude awakening. Single adults want to determine their own program.

The point is, a conscious decision to be involved in a singles ministry is essential! The remainder of this book describes some of the ingredients and implications of the deciding process. Where does a congregation start in making the decision? The first thing to do is learn a bit about singles; know some of their characteristics.

A congregation ought to find out how many singles are in the area. Without some singles, it is hard to begin a singles ministry! Where does one find singles? Some answers to these and other questions can be found in statistics about who lives where. These data often are available in or through the local library. However, some churches need only to look at the congregation in order to see singles in their midst and in their area.

Other pieces of data may come from a survey of what is available for singles in the area. This takes a bit of time and some conversation, but it does help the congregation determine if it can provide meaningful experiences for singles who live and work in the area or who already attend the church. Knowing about singles, their life patterns, their numbers, and their interests is essential to getting a ministry started and/or making an existing ministry more interesting.

Singles in Your Congregation

Suppose a congregation decides to take the first exploratory step in developing a singles ministry. This means looking for facts.

Getting facts about single adults is not difficult. The first place to look is within the church membership. Take the membership roll, gather the pastor and three or four others who are knowledgeable about the membership, and make a list of all known single adults. Limit the list to resident members (those within commuting distance) who are between eighteen and fifty years of age.

As names are added to the list, use some identifying codes to help categorize or group them. Entries of a small list might look like this:

Thomas Adams—D2, 0, 40s
16 Bone Court
Apt. A-16

Jill Bilit—D½, 3, 28
28 Court Place
Apt. 6-C

Judith Colint—W3, 1, 36

28 Court Place
Apt. 7-D

Henry Dreamer—NM, 0, 22
4 Down Street
Apt. 1-F

Maria Flomer—NM, 0, 29
126 City Avenue
Apt. O-61

The names and addresses are followed by a code which tells about the singleness, i.e., NM = never-married, W = widowed, and D = divorced. The number following the single status tells how long the person has been single. The next number tells how many children under eighteen years of age are at home and the final figure is the approximate age.

As an example, Tom Adams has been divorced for two years, has no children at home under eighteen, and is in his forties. Jill Bilit is recently divorced, has three children under eighteen at home, and is twenty-eight years old.

The kind of information desired and the codes to be used must be decided on before the list is started. The codes should be explained in writing at the top of each page of the list.

This type of list provides the information needed to make intelligent decisions about how many singles are in the congregation, their type of singleness, their family responsibilities, and their approximate ages. By the way, it is best to assume that each single works. It is more unusual for singles, including those divorced with families, not to work than the opposite.

After the listing procedure is completed, it is necessary to look at places in the community where concentrations of singles appear. For example, a city map for the preceding list shows Bone Court, Court Place, Down Street, and City Avenue each within three blocks of the church. A visit with the manager of each of the apartment buildings at these locations or a trek to the office of the city planner can provide the congregation with information about the probable number of singles in those buildings.

Exact numbers are not crucial at this point but an accurate estimate is important. For example, it is not necessary to know there are exactly fifty-one singles if a congregation can estimate, based on the fact that the apartments are all efficiencies and are fully rented, that there are approximately fifty people in them.

While the surrounding community may contain additional singles, the focus for making the decision will be the list of singles identified through the membership rolls. The kind of single adult that will be the target of the ministry will depend on the careful listing of people and information supplied by the small planning group.

The next step is to identify how many, if any, are active in the church and who can help serve on an initial planning committee. This is a critical step since this small group will determine the type of ministry to be established or if one is to be started at all. There is a strong correlation between the age and life status of the leaders and those who become participants of singles ministries.

Leaders plan programs to meet *their* needs. The programs, in turn, attract people with similar interests and desires. The choice of who serves on the planning committee will greatly influence who becomes the target audience.

If the congregation has done what has been suggested to this point, it has: (1) identified a group of single adults within the congregation and the community; (2) discovered within that group one or more persons who are willing to explore with others the possibility of starting a singles ministry; and (3) set up a core group which will be the planning committee. It is this planning committee which will work together over several months to plan for the first formal meeting.

It is important now to take a look at characteristics of singles ministries. This examination will enable the planning committee to make a more informed decision of whether a ministry should be started and, if so, whether it should be sponsored by this or several cooperating congregations. The use of this process by existing ministries enables them to evaluate their directions and target groups. No ministry should continue without some evaluation resulting in conscious decisions regarding directions and the type of group to be targeted.

It should be noted that the process outlined is useful no matter what program is being designed or what group is being discussed. The process would not apply only to a single adult program.

2

Decision Points Regarding a Ministry

Watching a group of young people approach a swimming pool is analogous to observing congregations becoming intentional about a singles ministry. A few of the young persons will jump right in without testing the water. Oftentimes they come up sputtering and will head for the edge. Other young people will put a toe in and decide the water is too cold for plunging; so they slowly wade in. Yet other young people will observe what is happening and decide not to go in but to sit and watch.

Establishing a singles ministry requires the same decision making process just illustrated. But a single adult ministry doesn't have to be a one-congregation affair. It can be jointly sponsored by two or more congregations. The key element in the sponsorship, whether a solo or joint effort, is intentionality. Assuming this, four decision points are important to consider before making the final plunge.

Size

Numbers are the big question for congregations considering a singles ministry. "Do we have enough people to be serious?" is not an academic issue. It is a question that needs to be faced and answered by every starting ministry and each one wanting to redirect the purpose and energy of an existing ministry. The base number for making a group worthwhile is the elusive figure.

No one can predict how many people will come to a given program much less estimate accurately the average attendance for a new or redirected singles ministry. Since no one has the powers of foreknowledge, it is necessary for the planners and leaders of singles ministries to set some size boundaries. These would give the leaders a range of numbers of potential participants as the leaders plan for programs, facilities, and future activities. Experiences from other groups are instructive in establishing these parameters.

"We just don't have enough people to make a ministry to singles worthwhile. I looked at our congregation the other day and there were just two or three there. That's hardly enough to start a ministry with."

"We had no idea how many people might come when we started. We thought there might be a dozen or so. We tried to play safe and had refreshments for twenty-five. Seventy-five people came that first night and it's been larger every meeting since. We couldn't have foreseen such interest by looking only at our congregation. Many of the people came from the area."

"How many did we start with? Our first meeting had nearly two hundred. I have never shaken so many hands or carried on so many separate conversations in my life. It was a revelation to us what the need was in our area. Our wildest hope was for about a hundred. We figured this was our maximum if everyone on our list brought at least one other person."

"We started with six and that's been the figure we have had for about a year now. Several of the original members have moved and new people have come but we have leveled off at half a dozen. It's a good size for us. We don't expect to get any bigger."

A congregation doesn't know how many people will attend and support a singles ministry. Chapters which follow will discuss ultimate size as a product of the leadership, purpose, facility, and program of a ministry. That's the *ultimate* size; at the beginning there is no way of telling exactly how many people these components will attract.

Don't worry about it. Begin with those who are available and interested. Give them time and support so they can become a group able to define its own program. Let them work out their destiny as a ministry.

If a church school class is the way a ministry begins, as few as two or three persons is acceptable. This may be too small a number for some teachers but it is a beginning. Some ministries I contacted had a regular attendance of half a dozen. While this may seem small, it was acceptable to the leaders. They felt the group's size was about what the subject matter and the teaching method could sustain. In these situations, if the class grew, a new teacher and/or a new classroom would have to be found.

If a group is focused on a particular type of single, such as the recently divorced, an effective program demands a minimum and a maximum number of participants. Setting the focus is a result of a survey and the development of a list of a core group. If the list of congregation members (the core group) doesn't meet the minimum size set by the planning committee, the planning committee must either revise the target or find a different approach to programming.

Setting boundaries on size is an important concept for planning committees to understand. The boundaries are the functional limits for a group given a particular type of leadership, program, and facility. Simply stated, the concept means a group cannot be smaller or larger than the boundaries if it is to accomplish the purposes set for the ministry. A church school class may have a minimum size of three and a maximum size of twenty-five. Beyond either of these figures the class cannot function in the manner envisioned by the planners or the leader. In the same way, a Sunday night dinner at the church would not be feasible with fewer than twenty-five or more than two hundred people attending.

The size range is based on the type of group, the kinds of programs, the facilities available for its meetings, and the leadership. Each of these is a factor of size. These factors need to be carefully considered as a group is being targeted and a meeting place selected (see chapter 4).

Once boundaries are set by the planning committee, it is necessary to work within that size range. If the actual attendance is larger or smaller than the feasible size, a reconception of the ministry is needed. It cannot continue to function as originally planned.

Setting boundaries is an effort to cut down the ''unexpecteds'' in a ministry's formation or reformulation. After a ministry has been around for a while the boundaries can be revised but this takes a few meetings of the singles group. A base number will begin to emerge of those who are interested in various types of programs and activities. Three or four months after a new ministry begins or a reformulated ministry has started, the planning committee might wish to change the size range and develop new program goals.

Cooperation with Others

An ecumenically-sponsored singles ministry is more effective in some places than a ministry sponsored by an individual congregation. The processes of getting started, deciding on a target group, working on the program, and recruiting and training leadership are the same for each. The major difference is that more time is needed to lay the foundation for the ecumenically-sponsored ministry. This is because of the difference in functional styles of the sponsoring congregations in making decisions and gathering support.

Three models of ecumenical ministry appear to be the most common. As we review these, it is important to remember that most singles ministries are, practically speaking, ecumenical. Nearly all of them have people from a variety of religious backgrounds and church memberships.

The first model of ecumenicity happens when *the need is greater than a sponsoring congregation can meet by itself*. Typically, a congregation decides to sponsor a singles ministry, goes through the planning, gets it started, and holds the first few meetings. The response is so great that the facilities and leaders are not able to cope effectively. The minister or one of the leaders approaches one or two nearby congregations for help.

This approach usually results in an agreement about some type of joint effort. The originating congregation may be content with this new sponsorship, or it may decide to focus very narrowly and start another group while assisting with the ecumenical ministry. This dual role works well when the group which the congregation itself sponsors is limited in size and its ministry is carefully defined.

A second ecumenical model occurs when *ministers in two or more congregations feel a singles ministry is needed in the area and begin discussing the possibility of starting one*. The motivation for the conversations could be approaches from singles in the congregations. However the idea starts, these two or more ministers talk with others who are involved in singles ministries, look through their membership lists for singles, and discuss their idea with a few singles. Following this informal exploration, they call a meeting with other ministers who have expressed an interest and at least two singles from each of their congregations. The meeting is chaired by one of the clergy or a single who has been party to the preliminary data gathering.

The purpose of the meeting is to test the group for interest, obtain commitments, and design the next steps to study the feasibility of the project. The first purpose of the meeting is met when each congregation makes a decision to become involved, though each congregation may not make a commitment of direct financial aid. For example, one church may provide the building, another can be responsible for handling the publicity, and a third may assign an associate or assistant minister to the project for a short time. In addition to these commitments, a small planning committee ought to be established and a target date set for a first meeting of the proposed group.

The planning committee functions like that in a congregation. The one difference is that it will meet more often to give itself time to share information with the involved congregations. Ecumenical decisions take longer because of the various ways of making commitments which congregations have.

This type of sponsorship may continue for some time. Other congregations may become involved while a few of the original sponsors drop out. It may become apparent later that the group is predominantly from one congregation. This may result in that congregation's assumption of responsibility for the ministry.

A third ecumenical model is a *shared effort for special purposes*. This type occurs when several congregations are sponsors of their own singles ministries, each with clearly defined purposes and target groups. The singles groups, perhaps by accident, may discover it makes sense to sponsor jointly some events or programs. A weekend experience, a hiking or camping expedition, or a seasonal party are the kinds of extras which could be sponsored by these several groups. The ministries, not the congregations, feel the need for this ecumenical endeavor.

No matter who starts the idea or is the sparkplug behind it, this kind of ecumenical activity is broadening and not threatening for the singles groups involved. It increases their opportunities for different kinds of activities, gives the leaders of the various groups a chance to become acquainted, and permits members of the different ministries to meet others whom they might otherwise not know.

A coordinating committee is essential to make this kind of ecumenicity work. The committee must be sensitive to the charge that it is taking over programs and leadership from particular congregations. The activities and programs which the committee plans should be designed to draw members from sponsoring ministries as well as individuals who might not attend any singles ministries. In this sense, the ecumenical venture is an outreach sponsored by the participating singles groups.

An ecumenical ministry can have a strong, positive impact. It gives people from several congregations chances to interact with one another. It affords small singles groups opportunities to participate in larger groups. It also gives those congregations which cannot sponsor a singles ministry an option for their singles.

In some communities the singles may not be church-oriented and not reachable through normal church channels. An ecumenical ministry might be started to address itself to a specific group of these singles. One or more units may be focused on young adults, divorced persons, widowed people, or career singles. The effectiveness of the ministry depends on its targeting and work with a particular group. The purpose is to reach the unchurched.

In other communities the singles groups of congregations may be small with most of them operating as church school classes. It would be helpful to organize an ecumenical ministry to provide opportunities to pursue special interests, such as hobbies, theater parties, picnics, and the like. The ecumenical ministry might also sponsor special progams for short periods using a resource person not affordable by any of the groups individually. The aim of this kind of ministry is to supplement the programs available through the separate groups.

Ecumenism is not all goodness and light; it has its problems. A major difficulty occurs when one congregation with a strict theology demands that all others accept it before cooperation can begin. The result is no cooperation! When a strict theological agreement is not made a requirement for cooperation, most singles ministries can participate with one another ecumenically.

Authority is another issue in cooperative ministries. Sometimes agreements are made in the past, acted on in the present, and are strained in the future. Conditions change and so do people. Authority has to be spelled out in documents that bind participants in an ecumenical ministry. When changes are necessary, they must be formally documented. Authority must not be administered casually if it is expected to be effective.

A third problem can occur in the area of funding and feelings of "ownership." Most congregations have a feeling of ownership when a ministry is sponsored by their churches. When the ministry is jointly supported, ownership by each congregation is lessened. This is especially a problem when one of the early supporting persons is lost and the church from which she or he came has no other active or supportive member in the ministry.

One leader described his experiences with an ecumenical ministry only in terms of finances. He said, "It's always a struggle to find the money to keep going. I have to do it and to be frank, I'm tired. It's the same problem every year and my energy level is getting thin. If only someone else would help out. But they won't."

A fourth problem is recruiting leaders. The commitments of leaders tend to be in their own congregations. An ideal type of leader is one with no current church ties but with a history of work in the church. Some individuals, if they become divorced, feel much more comfortable not attending their former congregations. These people can make very good leaders of ecumenical ministries because they combine interest with experience in the church.

Leadership Responsibility

Finding adequate leadership is another decision point for a ministry. The process depends in part on who initiates the singles ministry idea. If a small group of singles approaches the minister asking his or her help in starting a ministry, this group can become the core of the planning committee. Clearly the people in this group are interested, have motivation, and are willing to take the first step.

If a pastor recommends that a ministry be started, it may be unclear to the church who is to be responsible for finding and training the persons to lead it. The obvious assumption is that it is the minister's job; but a singles ministry should not rest completely on his or her shoulders. Pastors need to appoint and share tasks with members of a planning committee. If this cannot be done, the frustrations of both the pastor and the singles group grow. The pastor is not able to do justice either to the group or to the congregation. Time and energy demands are too heavy.

If a congregation makes a tentative decision to begin a singles ministry, the next part of the decision is to find a group leader. This person must be accountable to the congregation and should work well with the pastor. It may not be necessary to *hire* a person—a volunteer can be just as effective. Regardless of who is secured, a job description must be developed which spells out duties and accountabilities very clearly. (Leadership will be discussed in detail later on in this book.)

The congregation's decision must include an agreement to relieve the minister of some usual duties to help get this ministry going. This means allowing the pastor more time for outreach and consequently accepting the fact that he or she will have less time for members. Such agreements ought to be put in writing and authorized by an appropriate committee of the congregation.

Ministries should not be undertaken haphazardly. Energy and time will be needed to lay the foundations, make the contacts, and get the ministry operational. Some congregations, knowing the effort necessary, hire specialists for the six to twelve months it takes to get a ministry started. During this period mechanisms have been constructed, in the church and in the group, that can supply mutual support and organizational nurture.

The Planning Process

Planning means defining a target population, setting size boundaries, developing a procedure for leadership recruitment and training, and designing program possibilities. While these are set before the first meeting, subsequent experiences can change any or all of the parameters. A written record of both the original and changed parameters is a necessity.

Any lack of clarity about the purpose or strategy to be used in the ministry will lead to confusion and a directionless program. Effective ministries need to take the time to discuss carefully possible directions and types of groups before finally deciding on their target and starting the work needed for those first meetings. The group that has planned well continues to function for a long time. The group existing on a week-to-week or month-to-month basis has trouble keeping leaders and designing programs which are interesting. They just aren't attractive over the long haul.

An outside group (separate from the planning committee), such as a church Board,[1] after making a decision to have a singles ministry, must not assume it will suddenly appear. It will take time. The Board should give the planners at least a year to set up a list, do program planning, and hold the first meeting. The Board should not rush the process; nevertheless, accountability means regular reports of what is happening during that year.

[1] Individual churches will need to apply this term to their own congregation structure. The word "Board" throughout the book will refer to the governing board of the church or, in a multi-board structure, the board whose responsibility such a ministry would be.

3

Characteristics of Single Adult Groups

A bout half of our people come or go every three months. Single adults are very mobile.''

"In groups of 'single-again,' especially the divorced, people come only as long as they need to get help. Once they get through the crisis, they drop out.''

"We have a Core group and a Visit group. The Core group is usually small and can be counted on as regulars. There is another group which sees our ads, hears about us from friends, receives our newsletters, and comes for special events. We may not see them for months, but then they show up. We call them our Visit group.''

Each singles ministry is unique. Participants' circumstances, such as divorce, widowhood, or just plain singleness are marked by the diversity of their personal experiences. But singles ministries nevertheless are alike in important respects. While any given group can generate unexpected moments of accomplishment and despair which defy general trends, one can pick out characteristics and needs which are common to singles ministries.

A knowledge of the concerns common to singles ministries provides congregations contemplating the start of a ministry or evaluating one that is already in operation with an opportunity to test their expectations against realities. Among the common characteristics which must be dealt with are: singles' mobility, the competitive demands on their time, and their skepticism of the church. Because of these, every singles ministry needs to provide for both long-term ministry and short-term program planning and to find the quality of leadership needed to make the ministry effective. Within each of the commonalities are inevitable variations which come about because of the size of the group, general age level of the participants, and the style and interests of the leader.

The size of a church singles group may vary from half a dozen to a couple thousand people. It is apparent that the opportunities for personal involvement in a variety of experiences increase as the size of the group grows; yet the desire of singles to deal with certain issues is constant regardless of the group's size. While larger groups are able to offer more diverse programs because they have enough people interested in hiking, photography, ceramics, and theater parties to make these activities well-attended, the basic concerns of singles which revolve around living as a single in our society are the same regardless of the group's size.

"The younger singles, those in their twenties, are always on the go. They want to be active in sports or in other things requiring physical energy. Their schedules can get hectic. On the other hand, our older singles, those from about thirty-five upward, are more interested in things of a self-development nature. They like to be active too, but they're so involved outside the church they don't need so much here."

This generalization from a singles leader summarizes a difference based on age. The fact is that the needs of adults change as they grow older.[1] Career, purposes in life, and biological changes are factors in the shift in emphases among adults. While there are exceptions, different age groups require different types of programs and activities. This issue of age underscores the need for leaders to be sensitive to changing desires of singles.

One group, unless it is small (between six and twenty people) gen-

[1] For a popular discussion of adult life changes see Gail Sheehy, *Passages* (New York: E. P. Dutton, div. of Elsevier-Dutton Publishing Company, Inc., 1976). The bibliography provides other sources for more detailed study.

erally will not be able to attract all age groups nor all types of singles. A small group, like a small town, incorporates diversity and makes allowances for its members. A large group is more likely to separate into subgroups of like interests. Therefore, to be most effective, a ministry with more than twenty persons must carefully target its group.

Perhaps the most important consideration in any ministry is the leader. She or he will attract, because of personal interest and inclinations, persons generally like her or him. The ages of the leader and most group members will be similar, the reason for singleness (divorce, widowhood, never-married) of the leader and the majority will be the same, and the kinds of programs will reflect the interests of the leader.

No matter how well a singles group tries to plan and develop its programs to be inclusive of all ages and needs, the leader and the personnel on the planning committee will ultimately have much to do with the program diversity and the group's growth or decline. These differences in groups are discussed in more detail in a later chapter. At present we will deal with common characteristics since commonalities are the basis for the later discussion of how to work with variables in a ministry.

Mobility

A universal trait of singles ministries is the fluidity of their memberships. The only type of singles group where this is less of a factor is the one composed of widowed persons over forty-five years of age. Even they, however, often have the desire and the money to travel extensively. In this sense they, too, are mobile.

Mobility comes in at least three forms. First, mobility can be physical. This means moving one's household into an apartment or house, staying for a few months or a year, and then moving on to another apartment or house. This is the most common definition of mobility: repeated change in the living place. This type of mobility is most frequent among young adults, especially the never-marrieds who are establishing a career, completing school or some kind of training, or looking for a congenial living arrangement.

A second form of mobility is movement from one *group* to another. An individual may be a member of two or more singles groups, for example. He or she attends, on a specific evening, the group which has the most interesting program. Such persons may be part of the core group in one ministry, but they quite often go to other groups' meetings. Their leadership responsibilities in one group do not prohibit their attending other singles ministry programs.

A third form of mobility occurs when a program has successfully fulfilled the needs of the participants and they stop coming. This kind of mobility is most often found in "single-again" groups. Death of a spouse and divorce are specific crises in which people need help. They seek out a singles group which can address their problem, participate in it for a time (usually three to six months according to leaders of such groups), and move on. They may join other types of groups in the church, but their need for the singles group is finished.

These three forms of mobility are not identified negatively. They are encountered over and over in singles ministries. A few reasons for such mobility may help dispel the feeling among some leaders that single adult mobility is a curse.

Changes in a job or a career are factors which cause mobility. Single young adults are likely to be in college, technical school or graduate training, involved in management training, and/or working in their first or second job while experimenting with living styles. Even if they last two or three years, none of these experiences are long-term, although each has future implications. The psychology of young adults is based on short-term commitments; they do not think long-term. But they need the fellowship and support of others during the months and years of living in a temporary place and situation. A singles ministry can provide such transitional assistance as well as offer a long-term "home" to singles. While most singles cannot accept the long-term aspect, many will become intensely involved for short spurts.

Crises exact a special toll on personal commitments. Since a crisis is abnormal, it is unreasonable to expect individuals going through a divorce to establish a long-term relationship with a group. They cannot and probably should not. What they need is the support of a group which can help them answer questions about guilt, self-worth, love, and singleness. The help for their personal dilemma must be obtained in a short time in order for them to function well in society. Therefore, mobility based on need fulfillment during or immediately after a crisis is a necessary hallmark of a single-again ministry.

Another reason for mobility is newly found freedom and ability to travel. The travel may be by oneself or in groups, but freedom from the responsibilities which inhibit travel is valued highly among singles. They like the opportunity and take advantage of it, when their money permits, to get away from their normal routine. Some may take extended travel between jobs, immediately following a divorce settlement, or when the world seems to press in too much. Often they take off on weekends with work companions for the seashore, mountains, lake, or resort.

There are other factors promoting mobility but the point is that mobility is a way of life for singles. A ministry must be built and developed on the premise of fluidity of both members and leaders. When expectations of commitment are too stringent, the group will be unattractive to new members and will die from lack of new ideas. In one sense, single adult ministries require mobility to appear attractive and to thrive.

Fragmented Time

One of the problems in families is that of honoring a commitment to spend time together. Demands on family time are geometrically increased with each additional family member. If this is the case, single persons should have a lot of free time! Wrong! A single individual has no more control over time than does a family member. The culprits nibbling away at time may be different but they exist in one form or another for singles.

Work is a major drain on time whether one is single or married. Since most singles work, this is a constant demand of time. Indeed, the pressures for more involvement at work may be greater for singles than for marrieds. Singles are perceived by their employers to be freer to travel for work, to work late and on weekends, and to plan and work on extra office functions. All of these require time in addition to work hours, time many singles would normally consider free.

The developing and maintaining of multi-relationships is another type of activity unfamiliar (at least in its intensity for singles) to many marrieds. The need for secure ties with others while not becoming encumbered with long-standing or unwanted obligations is a delicate balance sought by many singles. Finding compatible people and working out relationships with them means testing people and groups so that mistakes will be of minor consequence rather than emotionally trying. Most of the testing and cementing of relationships is done in bits here and there over several months. This has the effect of chiseling the time of singles into fragments. A new fragment is made in the form of each added commitment however limited in scope it may be.

Another factor in time use is that of keeping family ties intact. For some young adults who have never been married this means visits "back home" which may require travel. For others, it means visits home of more frequency because of their proximity to their families. For still others, the demands of family may be related to dependent children. The latter situation carries with it constant time demands quite similar to those on married persons with children. The difference for a single parent is that he/she has no partner to share time with the children; the single parent must be all things to each child.

An expectation by leaders that singles ought to have total commitment to a ministry is not realistic. Singles don't have the time. Indeed, singles may have less free time available for ministry programs than do married persons. Singles, as well as married people, often takes courses in self-development or follow interests and hobbies. This takes additional time even though the courses or hobbies may be short-lived. While they pursue these interests, regular attendance at a singles group is difficult. This may be true for a number of weeks or a couple of months.

Loyalty should not be determined solely by the frequency of attendance at meetings. Loyalty is an attitude. People come when they feel it is possible. At times they become emotionally worn out and must drop out of many things, including a singles ministry. It is necessary for the church to be as tolerant of singles as it is of longtime faithful church members when these occasions occur.

Involvement in a singles ministry is an *alternative* use of time for most singles. It replaces other commitments and responsibilities rather than filling empty time. Singleness does not give people more time for activities. It makes them rearrange their schedules. They usually don't need the church to try to fill up their schedule with programs and activities. Most already have a full schedule.

When a ministry is developed with the understanding that it must compete for the time of the single participants, greater efforts are made to be creative and innovative. The ministry assumes, correctly for most singles, that the program has to be designed for busy people who will find time to attend interesting and worthwhile events.

Competition for the time of potential participants has led many ministries to use a tenure system for their leaders. Most congregations are familiar with tenure (an upper limit on time of service) and have such a system for service on committees and boards. The normal tenure is set at three years or two terms. In a singles ministry, a term may be as short as three months! Successful ministries require most participants to become active on a committee or subcommittee. Informing potential committee members of the length of tenure is an inducement to participation. Persons are made aware that it is acceptable to serve for only a short period of time.

With a short tenure system, assignments may change two, three, or four times a year. No wonder the issue of having a strong and continuing leadership figure behind the ministry is crucial! If the participants and leaders of a ministry are changing every three to six months, a congregation serious about maintaining a singles ministry needs to have someone on staff or to find a volunteer who can function as the continuing leader. This person provides the needed continuity in leadership, plans with the other leaders, and takes care of the details essential to any program effort.

The discussion of singles' fragmented time underscores the need for a congregation interested in a singles ministry to have one or more people who can enable the ministry as well. This individual, couple, or staff member must be able to assist persons who have only bits of time to plan programs and care for the mundane matters of group survival, but who still want to have interesting, competitive programs.

It is not necessary to hire a staff member to perform this enabling function although many larger groups find this addition essential. Many small groups work quite well with dedicated volunteers. The requirements of an enabler are time, skill, and commitment. A congregation must have a person or several persons of this kind or the ministry will be short-lived.

Couples often perform this function for singles ministries. It is not necessary to rely solely on singles for continuing leadership. The requirement of a ministry is that its programs are planned for and by singles. Several ministries which I contacted were enabled by couples. In other singles ministries, one or two singles willing to give a large amount of time and energy performed the enabling services. The singles who did this had a strong investment in their group. Several had been quite active in other church programs prior to joining the ministry as singles-again.

An important decision point for a congregation considering a singles ministry revolves around the ability to find the behind-the-scenes person or persons. These persons will not be the meeting leaders so much as the underpinnings for the group's life. Their function is essential since most singles do not have the time needed to do these tasks. I will discuss this further in chapter 6.

Skepticism

"Singles, especially young adults, are skeptical of the church. They feel it is not interested in them, does not understand them, and makes unreasonable demands on them."

"The people who come to the church are leery of it. They don't trust it, probably because of past experiences. It takes a while for them to feel comfortable."

"We make no bones about being church related but we make no specific doctrinal demands of our participants. We are not narrow or exclusive in our spiritual emphasis."

How does a congregation overcome the skeptical hostilities of singles, both the never-married and the singles-again? "Carefully" and "Over time" are the twin answers given by leaders of singles ministries! No effective singles ministry denies or waters down its church relatedness; it provides spirituality but not doctrinal overkill.

Many people interested in a singles ministry are secular oriented and have probably developed a great degree of self-reliance. They are thinking people who are skeptical about many things, including the church. In order to deal effectively with such individuals, churches must be honest and direct and must understand their own beliefs while being accepting of others' non-belief. If these qualities are not present, a singles ministry will not overcome the skepticism of potential participants.

One of the dangers to singles ministries is an insistence by congregations that a group be founded on narrow doctrine. The key word is *insistence*—to put it in a phrase, "Everyone must believe the same way." It may turn out that participants are homogeneous in belief. More likely, participants will include a few believers, a group of seekers, and several nonbelievers. It would be unfortunate to turn away the seekers and nonbelievers by demanding they all become like the be- lievers if they wish to remain in the group. This is being narrowly insistent on doctrine.

In many ministries, church school classes are an integral part of the program. These classes are based on Bible study with the curricula written by the leaders. In fact, one large singles group is built around Bible study on Sunday morning. It meets in a non-church setting. The aim of the study is to provide a basis for developing beliefs by singles without all the trappings of a particular denomination.

Long-Term Ministry Planning

"We have a planning group of six to ten people who meet monthly for program development."

"Every three months we give out an interest finder to see what kinds of things we need to work out programs for."

"If something doesn't look like it's going to go, we change it right away. We don't waste time because we would lose our group."

Ministry planning is essential! A ministry doesn't suddenly appear with successful and well-attended programs. It takes a lot of work. People who have the skills and are willing to help develop programs must be found and persuaded to do the planning. An important task of a congregation interested in a singles ministry is to help find such individuals and provide resources for their training.

How does a singles ministry go about its planning? The choice of a particular method would depend on the group's size and needs, though two patterns seem to be important.

1. The first pattern, advocated by most leaders regardless of group size, begins the ministry around a core group with whom the pastor or an appointed staff member can work well. A comfortable relationship between the group and the pastor appears to be essential. In the long run, a group, even one with associates or other staff assigned as liaison, needs the support of the senior pastor. Her or his roles are interpretation of the ministry to the Board, pastoral counseling for some participants, and occasional suggestions to the planning group for programming. The minister maintains a relationship with the planning group directly even though she or he may meet infrequently with them.

2. An insistence on regular planning sessions involving the partici- pants is the second pattern seen in many ministries. Planning needs to

be practiced if it is to help the group. The effective ministries receive input on a regular basis from the participants about programs and activities. When members realize the planning sessions are for their benefit, they respond and generate the rough program ideas which leaders can refine later.

These two patterns of planning are used by most successful singles ministries. They are general guidelines which any ministry, whether for singles or not, would do well to incorporate. Following are three models for involving participants in planning.

a. In some groups a short or partial session during a regular meeting time once each month or every two weeks is for planning. This may occur during the first part of the meeting or be sandwiched between other activities. The leaders take the data collected during the meeting and, at some later time, meet to screen out the suggestions which are not feasible and to work out the specifics of the programs that are feasible. This method allows leaders to circulate interest finders (See pages 15-46) and suggestion sheets and in other ways solicit program ideas from members.

A problem facing most ministries is the reluctance to change program format and direction. Change is an essential ingredient in life. Collecting new ideas from participants helps immensely in generating appropriate change and is a means for involving new people immediately in the group.

b. In larger groups, a subcommittee is assigned responsibility for planning programs for a certain number of weeks or months. Its task is to plan programs which are content-oriented as well as to plan recreational and social activities. In some very large groups, each of these three aspects of planning may be handled by different subcommittees. The use of interest finders, a careful selection of the planning committee to represent a cross section of the group, and stimuli from the leaders are needed if interesting programs are to be developed. Specific responsibilities must be assigned so the programs will be carried out.

c. In relatively few groups a staff person or singles ministry leader is responsible for planning all the programs. This, in some cases, includes writing, designing, or adapting curricula. The curricula may be Bible study, psychologically oriented sessions, or whatever the leader feels the content portion of the program may require. In most small group situations, the leader does not have a formal planning group and the ministry is dependent on the ability of the leader to come up with interesting programs. The group itself plans, during a part of its sessions, social and recreational activities.

Each of these planning models must be developed around the needs of the group and the aptitude of its leaders. The models depend on the blend of the people in a particular ministry but can be tested and used in other groups. When one planning model doesn't seem to work, another one might be just right.

It is usually necessary to change planning models or adjust the style when there are changes in staff or group leaders. Such changes should be regarded as normal and not be viewed with alarm.

A practice in many ministries is that of using an interest finder as a basis for program planning. An interest finder is a short questionnaire on which are listed various activities and interests. Individuals are asked to check items which appeal to them as possible programs or as a basis for setting up interest groups. The form may include opportunities to volunteer for committee work as well.

On page 46 is an abbreviated example of an interest finder. The interest finder must reflect the possible activities for the group. In this sense, it must be realistic.

It is not necessary to put the volunteer section (Section C) on this form; sign-up sheets may be used at specified times during the year. Instead of using either of these volunteer formats a group may ask a person to serve as chairperson of a committee. It then becomes her or his task to recruit others to serve on the committee.

The interest finder is easy to type up and can be run off on a copier or a duplicator in minutes. Sections "A" and "B" of this form can be used as given. If the volunteer section is included, preparing the form will take more time because it will be necessary to tailor the possible jobs to the particular group. Of course, you may want to tailor sections "A" and "B" as well.

Completion of the program idea section provides guidance to the planning committee. If this type of form is filled out every two or three months, the planning committee can evaluate directions in which it has been moving as well as keep current with the desires of the group. Use of these forms also is a means to become aware of quick shifts which happen when a major event creates a change in the thinking or composition of the membership. Since many ministries report significant personnel turnover every half-year, regular use of an interest finder is quite important.

The frequent use of formal interest finders is not essential in small groups. The leader can make informal inquiries on a random basis to test interests and directions. This relieves her or his tendency to do the same thing over and over because "it works well." Effective leaders, however, suggest using a questionnaire once in a while in order to be sensitive to the current needs of the group. People who are not forceful enough to make comments directly may write them down.

A. PROGRAMS (Rank 1, 2, 3, etc.)

_____Self-development
_____Skills: auto repair, home repair and maintenance
_____Money: management, banking, investing
_____Child care by single parents
_____Job hunting, job changing
_____Other:
_____Other:

B. INTERESTS (Check any or all)

_____Dancing (specify type):   _____Hiking
_____Swimming   _____Skiing
_____Camping   _____Writing
_____Horseback riding   _____Canoeing
_____Drawing/painting   _____Other:
_____Other:

C. I WANT TO WORK ON THE:

_____Planning committee   _____Arrangements committee
_____Social committee   _____Recreation committee

NAME:_____   ADDRESS:_____
PHONE #:_____   _____

A change in mood incorporated into programs during the past year has been a movement away from a totally psychological emphasis to that of providing a spiritual basis for single adult living. This new emphasis is based on Bible study. The shift may reflect new leadership capabilities as much as changes in people's needs. It is more likely that the change has been initiated by the participants' desires since most of the leadership I contacted has not been changed during this period.

The points to underscore about planning are: (1) planning is essential so that single adult programs can be responsive to the needs of participants; (2) planning involves both leaders and participants; (3) planning requires the collection of information about the interests and desires of the group in the areas of program content and social and recreational activities; and (4) planning done by one individual for a group must be informed by feedback from the group members.

Short-Term Program Planning

An effective singles ministry is one which attracts busy people and gives them programs interesting enough that they come back for more. A program is not measured only by its content: The caliber of a program is determined by its content, the atmosphere or environment of the meeting, and the group's leadership.

Ministries using the church school class as a primary meeting place and time usually develop their own curricula or adapt the curricula available through denominational publishing houses. Their sessions often begin with an exposition of the material under discussion by the leader. The format can adjust to the discussion of a topic of major concern of the participants if this appears to be more useful. In this sense, the class is a foundation-laying experience which assists singles to explore ideas and feelings in a non-threatening way.

The church school class approach is useful only when the material does not require acceptance of a narrow sectarian doctrine. When sectarianism is the aim of a single adult group, it eliminates the possibility of reaching those who are struggling with decisions, the solutions to which are not absolutes. The best type of class experience is reflected in a participant's comment, "It is a place to go where I can deal with personal issues in a constructive, non-threatening way. It is a religious experience for me even though I don't consider myself a religious person."

Larger groups also use the Bible study approach. In these cases, the curriculum is developed by the leader and taught in conjunction with other activities. One example is a large group established by a person who worked out a Bible study program. There are table groups of ten to twelve persons each who are assigned a discussion leader. The people at the tables, at an appropriate time during the proceedings, engage in their own discussion of the materials. During the week, the main leader meets with all of the table leaders to go through the coming lesson. In addition, table leaders are required to attend regular training sessions so they can facilitate discussion. They are instructed to direct people to specific types of counseling assistance when that is needed.

Another aspect of this particular group is its emphasis upon volunteer service. Each participant is expected to volunteer time to projects within the metropolitan area in which the group is located. The group has a very limited social and recreational agenda since the participants are not coming for these purposes. They come for study and constructive involvement in service projects. They come also because they get to know others like themselves in small groups.

This illustration underscores the means whereby effective ministries are able to continue to function: (1) They have a distinctive purpose which separates them from other singles groups in their area. (2) They have a leader who is sensitive to the need to spread work and responsibility throughout the group. (3) They provide training to those selected to be leaders. (4) They keep their interaction units quite small.

Another singles ministry tries to vary its program so that each meeting has a particular purpose. A monthly supper meeting has a limited program which includes an opportunity to give suggestions for future meetings. One meeting each month is devoted to spiritual development, another to an issue peculiar to single adults, and another meeting is social. The aim is to meet a variety of needs each month using structured variety in programming.

Other ministries request their planning committees to develop programs on a three- to six-month basis. The programs may utilize resource persons for such topics as single parenting, dealing with banks and financial institutions, living creatively as a single, sex and the single person, and the like. The ideas for programs are collected through interest finders or are the result of experiences of one or more members of the planning committee.

A few ministries use the seasons of the year as a guide to programming, although this is more difficult. Seasons are more appropriate for social and recreational programming than for content programming. It is better to use interest finders and put suggested topics into various time slots rather than base the programs on the seasons.

Up to this point, consideration has been given only to the study content of the program. Equally important are the social and recreational activities. These range from monthly dinner meetings to small interest-group meetings once or twice a week. The size of the group makes a big difference in the variety and number of social and recreational programs planned.

Another factor determining the range of social and recreational activities is the kind of singles group. Younger persons like more active events while older adults are more inclined to events which demand less physical activity. Single parents are often restricted because of responsibilities for children. Money is a factor in most programming.

Social and recreational programs must reflect the desires and abilities of the group. While the need and type of social events are rather universal, i.e., dancing, dinners, and theater parties, the manner in which a particular group engages in its activities must be unique to that group. Large groups have found it important to break into several smaller units to program effectively for the different types of social and recreational interests of their participants. Thus, in one very large group, one unit may be for never-marrieds under twenty-five years and another unit may be for divorced persons thirty-five to fifty-five years.

Creative programming includes variety and speaks to each person at his or her need level. This requires work and sensitivity on the part of the planning committee. It is one of the reasons for insisting on regular planning and feedback.

A second essential in programming is monitoring the atmosphere in which programs are conducted. In this case, atmosphere doesn't mean the air and wind currents but refers to the feeling a person receives at the meetings or in later contacts. The mood created by the place of the meeting, the attitude of the leaders, and the attractiveness of the program all combine to create the atmosphere.

One of the leaders of a singles ministry said, ''I try to get to the meeting place about half-an-hour before anyone else arrives. I make certain the room is in order, the chairs are in place, and the coffee is on so it will be ready for the first arrivals, and the lights are on. In other words, I like to give the room a feeling of welcome. That's really important to singles.''

This is his way to create an inviting atmosphere. However, the meeting room is only part of the setting. Hear another leader: ''I try to be at the door and have three or four others going from group to group during the evening to shake hands and greet people. One of the major needs of singles is to be touched. It doesn't seem like much, but that handshake at the door has opened people up so later they could come and discuss some personal things. I believe that touch—and we emphasize the need to touch during our meetings and in social times— means a lot to the single. Just think, where else can they be touched without being asked for something?''

The attitude of the leaders is another ingredient in the atmosphere. If they convey the feeling ''Welcome! You count!'' singles become comfortable. They will spot the non-caring, mechanical handshake as quickly as it is offered. The leaders' attitude must convey a feeling of welcome and a desire to have this person as a part of the ministry.

The follow-up after a person's attendance at a meeting is another part of the group's atmosphere. Many groups use a weekly or monthly newsletter to keep in touch with their members. This clues them into activities, tells what some other groups may be doing which would be of interest, and gives personal notes of happenings within the membership. This is the most common type of follow-up and requires little of the participant. It is a non-threatening, non-demanding form of welcome.

Other groups use a ''buddy'' system. Regular members are urged to make phone contact with new attenders and help ease them into the life of the group. This works only as well as the mix between the two individuals. In some situations it works well and at other times it bombs. When this system is used, it is best to precede it with a training session or two for the group members. The training would spell out ways for members to be helpful without being pests or being too personal.

In other groups follow-up is done by phone by a committee. If an individual attends a meeting for the first time, his or her name is given to the committee. The committee contacts the visitor via newsletter or a letter of welcome which includes a brochure describing the purposes and goals of the ministry. A member of the committee tries to call the visitor just before the next meeting. This method gives the new person an overall acquaintance with the ministry as well as personal contact with an active member.

These methods for creating an inviting atmosphere work well in different groups. The methods succeed because those charged with follow-up responsibilities feel this new person can be an interesting and productive addition to the group. When these methods fail, the problem can be traced to persons not doing the follow-through or conveying a non-welcome attitude in the contacts.

Leadership

Atmosphere is created by the program, by the place, by the feelings generated by the group at the meeting, by the follow-up contacts, and by the leader. Perhaps the most important of these is the leader. Listen to one person underscore this.

"People of the same general age, with about the same interests, and having the same reason for singleness are attracted by the leader. It stands to reason. A leader programs things of interest to her or himself."

Groups are built around leaders much the way organizations take on the personality of their top executives. For example, a group of divorced people respond to a leader who has been divorced and has worked through the feelings surrounding it. They do not respond to a person who is married or never-married and is not sympathetic to divorced individuals.

Perhaps the most important identification characteristic of a group is the age of the leader. People decide whether or not to join a group according to how much younger or older they are than the leader.

"This group is too old for me. I want somebody who understands my situation in life. The leader is old enough to be my mother!" This comment explains why one participant dropped out of a singles group. It had nothing to do with the program (although the programs were designed by leaders who were older) but was directly related to the image created by the woman who was the leader. She was "too old" for this former member. She looked as if she could not understand the needs of younger singles. The decision was based strictly on age.

Contrast this attitude with the one expressed by a participant in another group. "The one thing that makes this program is the vibrancy of the leaders. They are a couple and are so alive! It doesn't matter that they are older because they have young ideas and young ways of putting things.''

The rule of thumb is that leaders attract people of similar ages. However, the quality of the leader is extremely important. It is possible to find leaders who can appeal to a multiplicity of age and interest groups. Such individuals are unusual and probably not found in most congregations. Therefore, the safest assumption is that the age of the leader will determine the ages of the participants.

Creative programming is the content of the meeting which is added to or detracted from by the social and recreational activities. When programs are developed on the basis of data collected from participants, they are more likely to be diverse and interesting. A program, in spite of good planning, is a victim or beneficiary of the place in which it is held, the attitude of the leaders, and the follow-up of newcomers. Finally, a program is only as good as its leader. When there is little enthusiasm or creativity among the leadership, a spirit of negativism will overshadow efforts by others who want to enliven things.

4

Important Considerations in Ministry Planning

The main reason I come? I came at first because I was looking for an alternative to the singles bar scene. I stayed because I found what I wanted, a group who cared about *me,* not just a bunch of people who wanted something from me.''

"Activity is not my need. I'm involved in a lot of things besides this group. I want to be where I'm considered important. My hang-up is I need to be appreciated as a person.''

"Loneliness is probably the reason I got involved in this group. You can be in a group and still feel lonely, like in bars or big groups. Here I know the people and we communicate about things important to me.''

Coming to singles groups is a search for something not found elsewhere. In the comments of the singles above, the search is for caring, feeling important, and finding others with whom to talk in a meaningful and helpful way. People need to feel wanted and appreciated. Families have a built-in need for the presence and contribution of each member. When a member leaves, both the family and the individual feel a sense of separation and the individual must find another group which needs her or him. A single may come to a singles group for this reason.

In this age of instant everything, nothing has been found to replace people's need to interact in a caring and supportive fashion with others. Singles are especially vulnerable in this search simply because they have to create and cultivate relationships which can provide such experiences. This is especially hard when the single wants to remain single.

A recent experience with a congregation illustrates this difficulty. I put a hypothetical situation before the members of a church's planning group. It involved a single man who wanted to become active in their church. My question was, "How can this individual become an integral part of the church's life?" Ideas and suggestions came very slowly. They had not wrestled with singleness as an issue before. Finally, in frustration, one man said, "Let's get him married. We can deal with him then! We've got lots of things for marrieds!"

This is an attitude in many congregations. It's hard for them to deal with singles because church leaders haven't thought about a ministry or program for them. Even if they have considered it, leaders seldom discuss a singles ministry in meaningful terms. They do not think of it as affording opportunities to develop caring and supportive relationships among *singles*. They often think of it as a place for singles to go so they can meet a mate.

People seek out singles ministries for many reasons; one of these reasons may be to find a mate. From the church's point of view, however, this should not be the purpose of the ministry. It is not the function of the church to be a marriage bureau. The church's task is to minister to people in whatever marital state they happen to be.

What does a congregation try to do in its singles ministry? It founds a singles ministry on three principles: (1) In the church, people ought to be caring and supportive. (2) The aim of ministry is to help people create relationships which allow them to grow, learn, and love in a Christian manner. (3) A congregation does not have the right or responsibility to coerce people to change their marital status.

These principles preserve the integrity of the congregation and of the individuals who participate in its programs. The principles underscore the unique nature of the church, which is a place to establish and nurture loving, caring relationships between people. Finally, the principles warn the congregation that its concern with people's marital status needs to be focused on ethical issues rather than cultural practices.

An Alternative

A beginning point for establishing or revising a church's singles program is to consider it as an alternative to other groups. Most non-church singles groups are established so that their members can have a good time. They engage in a lot of activity with many people but try to keep relationships on a superficial level. They do not want entangling liaisons. Their aim is to have fun.

Their main activities are parties, mixers, rap sessions for persons with particular needs, and weekly sessions of large groups of like-minded people who want to dine, dance, and "be friendly." Those who go to these events are looking for immediate gratification. They are not interested in anything more than brief pleasure with no long-term commitments. They want a release from loneliness.

Perhaps this is one reason many single adults come to a singles ministry with few signs of commitment. They have become used to short periods of intense activity followed by a time to drop out, collect themselves, and restore energy in preparation for the next round of events.

Perhaps this, too, is a motivating factor for them to come to the *church's* singles groups. They are looking for more in life than a good time and a few laughs. They, like the people quoted at the beginning of the chapter, are searching for substance. They want groups which take their inner needs and desires seriously while not asking them to be other than single.

Earlier we talked about competition for the time of singles. In the present context that means that the church takes the word "alternative" as a guiding light for the group's existence and life. One participant, explaining her attendance, said, "I come here almost every time but if there is a dance or special event of some kind offered over at another singles group, I go there. I'm not bound here. It is a group I like to attend; it isn't the only place to go."

The ministry at church is *not* the only place to go. It is an alternative to other types of groups. As such, it must compete with others for the time and interest of potential participants. One leader, talking about this, said, "You really have to have an attractive program and an alive group to keep people. They make a snap judgment about you and you either win or lose on that decision. We have to be better than others.''

This overstatement emphasizes the reality of having a membership not totally committed to a ministry. Any ministry is an alternative and, as such, is under a mandate to offer something distinctive in its programs and activities. This is a challenge and should be considered an opportunity. It gives a church a chance to be a church, i.e., to provide a setting in which people deal with life-expanding issues and concepts.

The singles ministry, to be an effective alternative, should be concerned with the total person and not focus exclusively on the teaching content of its meetings. In other words, the content as well as social and recreational activities ought to be seen as a total program offering. The social and recreational events should be qualitatively different from those of non-church groups.

This does not mean church singles programs must be deadly, drab, humorless, and no fun. The aim should accomplish what one leader claimed for her group. ''Programs are fun. We try to plan a variety of events which bring people together just so they can play. Parties are really great even though they are held in the church and no liquor is allowed. Oh, some people grumble but we tell them that's the way this group is and they accept it.''

The other side of the coin is that singles who come to the church *expect* the group to be different. They *want* it to be different as indicated by previous quotations of participants. Even the more secularized attenders are willing to put up with what is, to them, the somewhat restrictive conduct codes governing ministry activities. If such conduct codes were not in effect, their reaction would be similar to that of the visitor to a rather liberal singles ministry meeting who exclaimed, ''Hey! I thought this was a church-sponsored group.''

Conduct codes are not the only differences between secular and church-related singles groups. The basis for a ministry is to develop another opportunity for people to experience the power of Christ. The content of the programs, the meeting place, and the emphases in the discussions are all informed by the message of the church. For example, many church-sponsored singles groups engage in Bible study as the primary means of getting at issues such as marriage, sex, and responsibility from a Christian perspective. Other groups use church resources and church people as leaders for programs. All of the ministries take advantage of the pastor of the church as a leader and as a counselor. These are the major differences or alternatives singles find in a church group as opposed to a secular group.

As noted previously, a few groups have trouble attracting men. The church singles ministry appears to be an alternative for women but in some situations it doesn't have the same kind of appeal to men. One leader reported, "Most of our group are older divorced and widowed women, usually over forty. Once in awhile a man comes, but with all the women here he probably feels strange. Afer a time or two, most men don't come back."

Another leader described her ministry's tact when confronted with this problem. "We tried to look at the singles and their needs and decided we should work with women only. We do. Most of them are divorced with a few who are widowed. They come for about a year and then begin dropping out. By then they have gotten through their personal crisis, have found a continuing support group, and can function effectively outside of the group. In addition, a few have married. We just consider the group for women and focus our ministry in that direction."

This description illustrates *targeting*. The ministry does not try to provide an alternative for all singles but sponsors a focused program which the leaders feel can be effective. This church chose a group it discovered during its research phase prior to beginning a ministry. Its decision was to direct good programs toward that particular group. It went in search of these people, found them, and they came. The leader did not say the participants were members of her ministry only. She did note that the church was effective in helping these persons at a critical time as they were searching for new meaning in their lives as singles again.

People attracted to the singles ministry will not all be church members. As one leader explained, "Only about 40 percent of our people could be considered church members and not that many are members here. Most of our group have very tenuous ties to the church. They come because our program is good and it is related to the church. I can't give you any reasons beyond these."

A congregation developing or redirecting a singles ministry must decide how its program is an alternative to those already in the area. It must focus on the strengths of its leadership, location, and congregation, and base a program on these. Every congregation, because of the nature of the church, can be an alternative to secular groups. However, its program in singles ministry must be attractive, or the work and plans to get it established will be wasted. People must find content that is helpful in social and recreational activities which are appealing and "good clean fun."

Separateness or Togetherness?

A decision facing some singles ministries is whether to become multi-unit or remain a one-unit group. This is a dilemma not faced by groups with between six and fifty in average attendance at meetings. The leaders of groups this size can usually adjust programs to meet the needs of the participants. Some of the members will attend social and recreational events of other singles groups. Such attendance is not disloyalty; it is recognition of the limits to the social activity which can be maintained by fewer than fifty persons.

A decision to become multi-unit means the group is divided into smaller segments. These subunits can be constructed around interests, similar age groups, type of singleness, or, as in one place, on the basis of residence (the ministry was for a large metropolitan area). In some ministries, the decision sort of evolves as the group grows. Interest clusters, age groups, and types of singles gravitate together and become informal subunits. After this happens, the leaders have to make decisions about the nature of the large group and its overall aim. This is much harder to do once the little groups are formed because by this time they have a life and identity of their own.

If a group decides to divide into subunits, it reflects a previous formal or informal determination of the ministry's nature. For example, one group, contemplating its future, had to choose between growth or maintaining a smaller group of compatible people. It decided, consciously at this time, to keep itself small but to help a new group for another type of singles (recently divorced) get started.

The basis of the group's decision was an informal feeling at the beginning that members wanted a small, intimate group. In essence, once the group was established, they didn't want a bunch of new people coming in and changing the structure or nature of their group. They liked each other and were comfortable with their program. After the group had figured these things out, discussed them openly and agreed on them, they could choose to keep their group small but expand the ministry (adding new dimensions; here, a separate group for the recently divorced). They chose expansion as the least threatening to their group and as a method for furthering the church's ministry. They could sponsor and provide limited leadership during the organizational phase of the new group while maintaining their own structure and program.

This illustration of one group's choice points to an issue for singles ministries. What should be done? It may be desirable to bring new people into the group and let it grow in size. Another avenue is to do as the former group did: keep the group as it is and expand the total ministry by starting a new unit for a different target population. This decision to expand the total ministry can result in starting new church school classes or in revising and adding to social and recreational activities.

The decision time comes when the average meeting attendance is somewhere between fifty and one hundred. Even this figure can be misleading, however. The type of program affects the decision time for some groups. For example, a church school class might need to consider splitting when the regular attendance makes a meeting room too small. This might happen when there are thirty to forty per session. Even when the group breaks, it is important for the larger unit to have monthly or semimonthly social or recreational activities. These types of events with all the subunits coming together have a positive pyschological effect on the ministry.

This is one dilemma of group life. An effective group must make it easy for personal interaction to occur while remaining large enough to provide variety in program. It is even better if the group is big enough for the members to develop some common interest groups. If it is not this large, as some church school classes are not, members go elsewhere to fulfill social and recreational needs. They may belong to other singles groups or they may have a limited social agenda. The former is probably more true than the latter although some singles prefer a very small social group with whom they feel comfortable.

A continuing need for individuals, single or married, is to feel they belong to an organization which is alive. They expect it to grow, or at the very least, generate a flow-through of people. If new persons come to each meeting, the members feel attractive and desirable as a group. A danger of splitting the group into various segments is that of losing this feeling. This loss of a sense of attractiveness is intensified if the larger group does not meet regularly.

Members of a group that is considering dividing need to be sure that there are enough people who want to join each of the subunits to make them interesting and viable. There may be situations when a split results in one quite large and one small unit. This is acceptable if the two subunits are viable and meet together as a larger entity regularly. Most of the time splits can be made with a relatively even distribution of persons among the resulting subunits. Again it is important for them to be together for larger meetings which feature special programs, social events, and/or recreational activities.

A typical result of carefully considered splits is overall growth in the group. One leader tells what happens in his group. "People are attracted by those who belong. When they like the group and what it does, they tell others. There is sort of a snowball effect. That's the reason we have so many interest groups in the ministry. It gives more people an opportunity to get involved."

This can be said a bit differently from an organizational development point of view but the result is the same. When a ministry offers several avenues through which people might fulfill personal interests and become involved, it is very attractive. The more opportunities there are for becoming active, the more likely a singles ministry will be a magnet to singles. People come and participate if the program and group prove to be worth their time. This is important to keep in mind when beginning or revising any ministry within a congregation.

Up to this point, the discussion has revolved around numbers and growth. But what if a group remains at a constant size, say twenty-five regular attenders per meeting, even though it might attract seventy-five to one hundred different people in a month of meetings? Where does a group look for the cause of the flow-through? Is there a way to attract the transients so they become regulars?

These questions are common enough to deserve attention. Indeed, the questions are most often asked by ministries which have been functioning for a few years. They know they must be doing something right but they feel the flow-through is an indication of potential disaster. They are probably correct in this feeling.

Planning and keeping abreast of members' interests was a theme of one part of chapter 3. Let's underscore fundamental understandings about planning and research. It is not enough to *collect* information; the data must be used for *decision making* about the nature of the group, its programs, and the purpose of the ministry. Unfortunately, few groups take the time to work through their purposes and proposed audiences once they have begun the programs, even if the purposes are changed and the proposed audience is not the actual audience. Many ministries make small adjustments to accommodate to their real situations without formally changing structures, purposes, and programs.

Such constant and informal adjustment is a practical and commendable strategy for singles ministries. Yet effective ministries which are able to keep themselves attractive use research frequently and test their targeting of audiences regularly.

One leader, for example, described in detail the year of work he spent in identifying potential group members, analyzing the possible attractiveness of various types of programs, discussing proposed ministry directions with selected singles, and finding leaders—all before the first meeting was held. He had, on the basis of much work with a small committee, decided on a specific target group which, in turn, helped him define the possible programs.

The focus of that ministry was to be people between twenty-five and thirty-five years of age who had become divorced within the past year. This narrow-gauge singles ministry was the intentional target. After the second year, based on research and testing of audiences, the leaders decided to begin another group and not to expand the existing one. The new group would be for older divorced persons between thirty-five and fifty-five years old. Leaders also decided to work at developing a group for young adults, under twenty-five years, who were never-marrieds.

These leaders had looked at their flow-through and attractiveness and had made some changes in their planning. The result was the addition of two new groups. While there is no quick answer for any question involving a ministry, the careful collection of information, the use of the information to plan practical directions, and getting on with the task comprise a very helpful process to follow.

Reiterating the experience of this particular ministry, planners made a policy decision based on their original research and targeting, not to split or to grow randomly. Their aim was to offer programs and group experiences for people of similar ages who had a common reason for singleness. When faced with new data, the original concept was maintained and new groups were formed. The procedure followed by the group proves to have at least three advantages.

1. When a target group has been identified carefully, program content and publicity are easier to develop. Neither has to reach across a spectrum of social and content concerns for all types of singles. The track is narrow and focused.

2. Leaders who reflect the age and type of singleness of the group can be recruited more easily. In fact they will probably have been a part of the planning process. Since the leader attracts participants of similar age and interests, group growth is a benefit of careful targeting.

3. It is easier to know when to close out an existing group or begin a new one when audiences are targeted. In this book examples have been given of groups which have started new groups. The following illustration is of a group which found one of its targets gone.

A singles program was functioning very well in a community adjacent to an army installation. In one of the governmental cutbacks, the base was closed and the personnel transferred to another location. This meant a part of the total singles ministry, that designed for young adult never-marrieds from the base, was no longer valid and so it was terminated. The other aspects of the ministry relating to divorced and widowed individuals not on the base were not affected. These remained in operation. If the ministry had not targeted its groups, the loss of the military personnel probably would have wiped out the ministry.

To summarize: If a ministry finds itself having to work with one hundred or more persons at each meeting, it needs seriously to consider splitting into subunits. This means smaller units with separate leaders and different meetings with one general gathering a month or week. Division into smaller units will allow for social and recreational activities which are oriented to age and type of singleness. The ministry will be attractive through the subunit leaders and programs.

Much has been made of the need to establish groups which are relatively homogeneous. This is the meaning of targeting audiences. Evidence collected from singles ministries indicates that they narrow themselves into particular tracks. Even if a group wants to minister to everyone, it will eventually become focused by design or default.

Singles ministries are begun because of a need felt by a specific group. This group attracts others like themselves and the ministry is under way. If this group tries to expand into other age categories or types of singleness, it either changes the original character of the group or it does not reach the new people.

People identify with other people. If a ministry wants to be effective from its inception, it must take the time to identify who it wants to reach, why people will be attracted, and how they will become involved enough to be regular attenders. These are issues which should be dealt with at the beginning and at each regular review of the ministry's purpose and program.

It is best to develop several focused groups under a singles ministry than to attempt one which tries to include everyone who may visit. Targeting and focusing programs are two key elements to effectiveness in ministry. Broadside welcomes and invitations with nondescript programs frustrate the expectations of both visitors and leaders.

Meeting Time and Place

Sunday morning and evening are prime times for singles group sessions. The Sunday morning time usually involves church school classes or Bible study groups. Most of these are held in churches although there are exceptions. The church school classes may meet in annexes to the church building, the church's social hall, or unused classrooms. Many churches are not well equipped to handle another adult class and must find or make adequate space.

Church school classes offer the opportunity of attending the worship service. In some congregations, the class has become the vehicle through which singles begin to feel comfortable about being in church. In other congregations it is difficult for singles to feel welcome in other aspects of church life so their experience ends with the class. For some singles, the class meets whatever need they feel to go to church. As one participant said, ''I get everything I need out of the class session. I don't want to go to church because I've never liked it.''

A feature of some groups which meet on Sunday morning is an informal arrangement for those who desire it to have lunch or brunch together. This ranges from an informal affair for small classes to a reserved place in a dining room for large groups. The intent of this occasion is to increase the opportunities for companionship in a congenial atmosphere. Someone, usually the class leader, is responsible for making the arrangements for reservations or for contacting the restaurant to alert them to the number in the party.

Sunday night is another good meeting time for singles groups. In many groups a meal is served at limited cost. This is followed by a program and social time. Not only do the participants get a meal but also the financial stability of the ministry is assured since the profit from the meal is used for program costs. (Some groups have the meal and program format on nights other than Sunday.) Invariably attendance is good. Singles don't like to eat alone all the time and if the hour is chosen carefully, this event is quite attractive.

Interest groups which are parts of a ministry may meet on any evening since their schedule is determined by the members of each unit.

One issue faced in scheduling these groups, when the church building is the primary meeting place, is the availability of space at the time chosen for the meeting. The use of rooms must be cleared with the office in advance. This is the same procedure used when a church annex is used. If the groups decide to meet in homes, the place must be decided on and people contacted in plenty of time before the meeting. The use of facilities other than the church or homes may be involved. This should be investigated before the meetings are scheduled.

These comments are important because a ministry choosing times for meetings is partially governed by the schedule of the meeting place. If, as in some ministries, this means taking the hindmost of space and accommodations in the church, it is a good idea to meet elsewhere, although the church is probably the best place for meetings.

Smaller ministries often rotate meetings among the homes of members. This has the potential for creating a clique, and, according to leaders of such groups, it tends to produce a reluctance on the part of one or two members to have others in their home because they don't feel their dwelling places measure up. These kinds of problems are minimized when all meetings are held in the church or a neutral meeting hall.

Noon was set as the meeting time for one ministry for a specialized program. It did not draw enough participants to be continued. The problem with meeting during the working day is finding a time when the participants have time off from work. This doesn't always occur at noon.

A few groups meet weekly right after the workday ends, usually around 5:30 P.M. or 6 P.M. The members generally work in the downtown area of a large city and come directly from their jobs. The meeting place is close to the major arteries and is convenient to the downtown area. The theory behind the time and place is that once people disperse across the city to their homes they are not willing to come back. Also, there may be no other central location which would attract as many participants. This illustrates again the need to focus on an audience and then customize the arrangements for meetings.

Setting a time and sticking with it is important in order to keep people coming. "We use 11:00 on Sunday morning as the time for our meeting because it is sort of fixed in their minds that this is church time. We thought about other times but this made the most sense to us. People are creatures of habit so we just turned the habit to our advantage." This comment emphasizes a practical way to use habit to advantage in scheduling events.

On the other hand, it may be necessary to experiment with meeting times before something really clicks with the group. For example, one leader reported, "We used to meet on Tuesdays, but when we tried Fridays, our attendance doubled. We cut out the regular Tuesday meetings." When at first you don't succeed with a time, try something else. However, experimenting with the time can't go on for a long period or else people will get confused. Remember the comment about habit! Give a meeting time an opportunity to succeed before changing it. If it is necessary to make a change, let people have plenty of advance warning so they will be able to reschedule other activities.

Deciding on a meeting time and place is rather tricky. One group, after careful and thoughtful consideration, chose Friday evening for its weekly session. The attendance was dismal! This continued for a month; so the leaders took the issue to those who came. The participants suggested a Sunday evening trial. This was tried and the group grew. Even though the leaders had been meticulous in their research and planning, they discovered, as most of us do eventually, that plans must be reality-tested. Feedback from the members is essential, especially on the time and place of meetings.

Safe bets for meeting times appear to be: (1) Sunday morning (as early as 9 A.M. in some places), (2) Sunday evening, (3) Monday evening, and (4) Friday evening. Saturday seems questionable. Other evenings can be used for interest groups. Afternoons are useful only in area-wide ministries when the meeting place is downtown and the sessions are immediately following work.

These recommendations concern only the regular meetings. Weekend retreats and other special types of meetings are treated differently. In some groups, for example, retreats are scheduled four times per year while in others one or two a year are reported. Memorial Day and Labor Day weekends seem to be especially popular. Neither of these holidays are family-oriented and singles may be more free on these than on other holidays.

In addition to retreats, some groups schedule occasional "weekends away." These are outings and overnights for as many of the group as are free to go someplace for skiing, hiking, a theater party, or whatever. Weekends away take planning for the details of transportation and lodging. However, in some groups these outings are the extra spark which keep people coming back regularly. The cost for these events is kept low and is borne by those who attend.

Program Focus

A program's focus can be positive or negative. Church leaders normally don't think of programs in these terms but this is a good way to look at a singles ministry. The nature of a ministry is based on the underlying focus or attitude of the leaders, which can be either negative or positive.

For example, one leader talking about the singles-again ministry with which he works said, "We constantly have to direct the emphasis to a positive note. If we didn't, we would end up wallowing in our guilt and hurt. We have to be hard on the members so they can change their outlook and get the skills they need to cope with life. I'll tell you, it's a struggle."

Apparently this is not an isolated situation. Programs can concentrate on people's problems, or programs can look at opportunities resting within problems. This latter turns out to be the more effective and enriching way to develop programs. That's the reason so many ministries sponsor events or interest groups aimed at helping members develop new skills. Sessions to assist participants to learn how to do minor repairs on an auto, to get know-how and self-sufficiency in household repairs, or to expand abilities in art and writing are ways to make programs positive. Sessions with experts who deal with issues of self-worth, self-identity, and the like are helpful and positive.

This need for a positive program focus was stated well by one singles ministry member who said, "We've gotten ourselves into a rut. We just talk about ourselves and our situations. It doesn't help other than to rehash past history. We need to get a different focus.''

The path of least resistance in programming is to concentrate on the common hurts and complaints of a group. This focus is needed for a while but in the long run it becomes self-defeating. While it is difficult, people must look to the future more than to the past. Singles, especially singles-again, must develop coping skills and attitudes which make them contributing members of groups and the larger society.

One way leaders can correct this tendency to keep a negative focus is to exchange ideas and experiences with other singles leaders. This is somewhat hard to do because a ''singles ministry directory'' is not yet available. A few singles magazines are available which are upbeat and give the experiences of others. Several denominations have staff persons in the area of singles ministries. They can listen and react to proposed program directions. A list of some of these resources· for exchange and contact is in the Appendix.

One criterion for all program suggestions and the activities of the ministry should be, ''Does this contribute to a positive attitude and focus within the group?''

If a group persists in being negative, as some do, it is a good idea to change the staff person relating to the ministry and/or find new leaders for the group. This will enable a congregation to redirect the program and focus. Usually a drastic measure is not necessary if a careful selection of leaders has been made and a limited tenure system is in place.

Monitoring by the pastor is helpful to leaders who feel things are out of hand but can't seem to make corrections. A pastor can help the planning committee evaluate and revise the program. Periodic meetings or a retreat are two ways to accomplish the evaluation. The reason for the pastor functioning in this role is that she or he is an outsider to the group but is sympathetic to the intent of the ministry and is familiar with the dynamics of the congregation.

These comments may be unnecessary in many ministries. Yet enough leaders felt boxed-in to prompt these cautions. Be alert to the possibilities of a negative focus and work hard against it. A singles ministry deserves to be more than a group which comes together to rehearse individual failures, defeats, and sad histories. People do have all of these but they have futures as well. The church proclaims the future and how one should prepare to inherit that future. This is a contribution of a singles ministry. Pastors may need to provide this positive corrective in particular situations.

5
Resources for Program Development

I develop the program on my own. I get the ideas from conversations, discussions, and suggestions from members of the group. I try to be sensitive to the needs of the members."

"We use every specialist we can get. Most of them are professionals like doctors, psychologists, counselors, or lawyers although a few are technicians and skilled people like auto mechanics, builders, and the like. We get our program topics from the participants and go find people who can address the issues. It works well for our group."

The heart of a ministry is its programs. Social and recreational activities are available in places other than the ministry. The distinctiveness of a ministry is what goes into its programs and how they are conducted. At the risk of being redundant, it is important to restate the principles which existing ministries use as they go about program development.

Perhaps the use of interest finders is the most common way to uncover topics and concerns close to the lives of ministry participants. The task of putting topics into programs takes time. Once a topic or concern is suggested, it must be considered carefully before it gets translated into a program. Planning for it will take many hours.

A planning committee has finished the easiest one-third of its job when it completes a three to six month program schedule. The other part of the work is: (1) to sharpen each topic to meet the needs and expectations of the group; (2) to find a leader for each program; (3) to give sufficient background and direction to the leader so she or he can do what is expected, and (4) to do the backup work such as publicizing the program, making facility arrangements, and assuring an inviting and comfortable atmosphere for the meeting.

After several years as chairperson of my church's adult education committee which is responsible for planning twenty-seven four-week courses per year, I feel that leaders are available for most kinds of programs a church may decide to offer. During the past four years, we have been able to find persons from the church who had the training, skill, experience, or jobs in the topics which were developed into programs. Experts and advocates from the community were another source of leaders. These kinds of leaders are generally experienced speakers and can provide good direction for most programs considered by a ministry.

The purpose of this aside is to reassure people who may be anxious about where to find leaders for a wide-ranging program. More will be said about leaders later, but it is important for ministries to realize that many leaders for programs are sitting in the pews or are friends and colleagues of church members. Never overlook this reservoir when thinking about leadership and don't be frightened into staying with just one or two topics in programming because you don't feel leaders will be available.

Steps in Program Planning

The development of a program consists of at least six steps. Each idea which is suggested will need to go through all six steps if it is to become a program. The work of program development is usually done by a planning committee, although it can be accomplished by one person.

The first step is to identify the needs and concerns of the group. Any one of these may become a program. The second step is to sharpen the need or idea into a definable program. The third step is to find a leader and the fourth is to advertise. Fifth is to check with the leader for needed supplies and the preferred room set-up. Finally, the leader must be greeted, last minute details have to handled, and the program helped to proceed as planned. When a committee has done each of these, the program should proceed smoothly. Now let's look at each step more carefully.

Step One: Identifying Needs

Needs which eventually will be programs are culled from conversations, discussions, personal feelings, and suggestions. While there are universal human needs, such as a sense of personal worth, a sense of self-identity, sex, and friendship, which can be worked into programs, most groups need to tailor these and other topics to address the specific situations of their members. For example, a group of newly divorced persons under thirty years of age will have different agendas and emphases than persons in their fifties who have been widowed for some time. The program topics and leaders may be the same but the emphases and the presentations will be different. Programs must be in touch with the people for whom they are intended.

Step Two: Translating Needs into Program Requirements

A feeling or hunch about a possible topic needs a lot of study before it can become a sound program. The hunch has to be examined, tested, and broadened so a program can be built. This involves defining the specific need to be addressed (this is called by some the *purpose,* or *objective,* of the program), narrowing the focus so the topic can be adequately handled during the time limits of the meeting, deciding on the appropriate slant or emphasis a leader will be requested to use, and specifying expectations about the results of the meeting.

This step is more crucial than any of the others. If this is not done well, the program will founder because the leader may not address the issue, may take off on his or her own agenda, will be unfamiliar with the needs and experiences of the group, and, in general, will kill the program. An illustration of how a committee takes an idea and molds it into a usable program may help.

Suppose the need for coping with everyday problems has been suggested as a program idea. The planning committee talks about it and tries to put some particulars into it from the perspective of the group.

For example, who will be doing the coping? What are the problems? What can be expected to be accomplished in an hour-and-a-half program? The answers to these and additional questions must be found by the planning committee. Following a series of committee discussions, it is clear that the need is for information about handling money, taking care of minor repairs on the house and car, and managing time. The program focus is for people who have recently become single again.

Now the committee is ready to make a series of decisions. The first is whether to try to cover all of these items in a single program or to have several programs scattered over a month or two of meeting times.

This is simple for most groups. They choose to have several meetings. Their final decision is to hold four meetings with each addressing a different topic.

Their decision about audience has already been made. The program focus will be for those who are newly responsible for all aspects of their lives because of a recent divorce or widowhood. The discussion around this decision was spirited and involved the question of who would come. It led to another decision to open these meetings to the community through invitations to other churches and singles groups.

The final decision deals with the choice of the leader. Who can discuss each topic, give some illustrations, and perhaps use personal experience in the presentations? The discussion concludes with the decision to use experienced persons who have talked to other groups in the church or community and to ask them to make their programs as practical as possible. They are requested to bring examples, tools, or diagrams which people can study and discuss.

These decisions come after much discussion within the planning committee. The decisions are based on a knowledge of the group and a sense of what is needed most by its members. Only after these choices have been made can the program take shape. Deciding on the specific topics, identifying the target audience, and setting the emphasis for the presentation must be settled before discussing the selection of a leader.

Step Three: Finding a Leader

Finding a leader is not as difficult to do as making the previous decisions. Once determinations about the program specifics have been made, a description of the kind of leader desired can be given. A possible leader for this program may be a member of the group or a friend of one of the planning committee members; he or she may be a resource person at another singles' group, a teacher in the community, a member in the church, or an acquaintance of a friend. In short, once a topic is narrowed so it can be a productive program, it is relatively easy to find an appropriate leader.

Step Four: Advertise

Most singles ministries grow and reach people because of personal recommendations. This informal communication process is more effective than any other form of advertising. People who belong are so enthusiastic about the programs and atmosphere of the group that they tell others. This gets the word out along the singles networks which seem to exist in every community. Along with this informal process, ads and activity listings in small neighborhood or community newspapers are quite effective in reaching those who might be outside the singles networks.

A few singles leaders have appeared on local radio or television talk shows. These occasions provide an advertisement for the group and what it is trying to do, but rarely are the specific programs discussed or announced. Since this is an occasional and sporadic opportunity, it is not a key factor in advertising for most singles groups.

A slightly less expensive way of advertising is to develop newspaper feature stories which tell about a particular kind of event or describe the group. These can be done by a member of the group or a reporter for a local paper. The use of the newspaper medium is important, especially in metropolitan areas. Local papers are less expensive for ads and are more likely to carry feature stories and activity listings than are metropolitan papers.

No matter the medium, ads must be directed to the target group or groups. If a program is for single parents, the ad should state this clearly. People need to know how they will benefit from the program experience, so it is important to be honest and factual in the ad. Potential participants don't want to be hoodwinked or embarrassed. This happens when people come to a meeting and find it does not match or live up to what the ad seemed to promise.

A singles ministry will, as a matter of course, keep its church and other churches in the community informed of activities and programs.

This usually is done through the church newsletter or a bulletin which is sent to members and friends of the church.

Most singles groups have a newsletter for their members. This is sent to those who visit as a means of introduction and follow-up by many groups. It describes upcoming programs, events of interest in the area, and plans for future undertakings. Some newsletters include news of members.

Step Five: Check with the Leaders

It is uncomfortable to come to a meeting and wait while the leader scrambles around for an extension cord, a pad of newsprint, or a slide projector, or sets up chairs for the audience. It is just as disconcerting to come into a room which has not been cleaned since the last meeting. Tables with splotched and torn tablecloths, debris in the corners, a broom leaning against the speaker's stand—all are distracting and contribute negatively to the atmosphere.

It is important to find out what the leader will need for the presentation and how the room should be arranged for the program. It is equally important to make certain the facilities are clean and attractive before the first participant arrives. It may be important, if this is not a meal meeting, to have coffee, tea, or soft drinks available as people come in. These amenities help create an atmosphere of warmth and cordiality.

A planning committee which leaves facility planning out of its preparations will have problems with attendance. A poorly organized facility can ruin a program. Let each leader assist in making the group's program run smoothly by describing how the room can be made most inviting for the topic under consideration.

Step Six: Be There

One of the most difficult beginnings for a program leader is to come into an unfamiliar group and not be greeted. The leader has probably had contact with someone in the group but perhaps that individual is not present and has made no provision to have the leader met and made welcome. The person who made the contact ought to be present to greet the leader. If this is impossible, the leader ought to be informed of who will meet her or him, and that individual *must* be there. This little courtesy gets the meeting off to a much smoother beginning.

It is important for this contact person (or the committee assigned this responsibility) to be at the meeting place half an hour ahead of time to set up the room. This may mean putting chairs in place, setting out refreshments, turning on lights, sweeping the floor, or doing a number of other little chores. It is much better to do these before the meeting so that the group can come into an inviting surrounding.

Planners need to plan the total meeting, not just the main event. This requires thought about opening remarks, business (if there is need of any), refreshments, informal time, games or recreation, and closing. Being aware of the sequence and keeping on top of the time and pace of the meeting is a key element of good planning.

These six steps are essential in the development and execution of each program. If one step is skipped, the results will be disenchanted participants, a disgruntled leader (one whose return you may want but who may be turned off by a bad experience), and a disappointed planning committee. Having been in this situation myself, I suggest it is better to take the time to work out these steps carefully beforehand so that the program will run as hoped. There are so many unexpected contingencies which can happen on any given meeting night that it pays to plan. This way, one will be prepared for other eventualities.

Finding Program Leaders in the Community

"Where do we get program leaders?" is a legitimate question yet is not heard very much from leaders of singles groups. They seem to have connections and are able to find the people they want to lead their programs. Some of their suggestions can be helpful to other groups.

Counselors working for private or public agencies are used often as program leaders. In some instances they are paid, but many are willing to come and lead a program without charge. These leaders can deal with subjects like: coping with feelings of self-worth, identity as a single, handling defeat, being positive and assertive, and a host of similar personal concerns. These leaders may be known to the pastor or to members of the planning committee. It may be wise to contact pastoral counseling offices in the area to help find leaders for such programs.

Lawyers are used in several ministries for programs, such as those on drawing up wills, the legalities involved in the custody of children or adults, the rights of a single, the handling of controversy, and other single-related concerns. Usually a congregation has a lawyer as a member or as legal counsel. If such an individual is not able to assist, she or he will help find others who can give leadership.

In some localities, law clinics offer workshops on topics of interest to singles. A few groups have been able to schedule special meetings around the workshops or have had a workshop scheduled as a part of the meeting.

Accountants, brokers, money managers, and bankers usually can arrange to be present for particular types of programs. They are especially helpful in dealing with money management, budgeting, establishing credit, tax problems, investing, and other issues involving money and the single person. In programs involving money, the leaders will need to begin with the most elementary steps of money handling because many singles have not had experience in finances prior to their present situation. This may be particularly true of the recently divorced, widowed, or the never-marrieds if this is the latter's first time away from home.

Sessions led by builders or contractors who discuss simple repairs to the home or apartment, energy efficiency, and what to look for in purchasing a home or renting an apartment are usually very helpful. In the same vein, mechanics can teach techniques of auto troubleshooting and simple repairs. These sessions are particularly helpful to singles who get caught in an emergency at home or on the road.

Community experts not often thought of are hobbyists. These people can provide programs of an informative or social nature. Square dancing, social dancing, ceramics, magic, painting, dramatics, writing, and other topics are among the interests of hobbyists. Hobbyists may not be widely known but can be found by asking the pastor for suggestions of leaders for these kinds of programs. An ad in the church bulletin or newsletter for a person with a particular skill is also effective. Most hobbyists will come for free and will spend time with the group. Their programs tend to be more interesting if the hobbyists know the level of knowledge and interest the participants have in what is being discussed or shown.

Another source of leaders are people who teach in the high school, elementary school, or college in the community. They can lead programs dealing with child development and specialities such as music, math, business, computers, bookkeeping, and the like. We have used English, music, business, and art teachers as leaders for adult programs. It is very important to define and focus the programs for which these persons are asked to be leaders.

In addition to the above resources are people who work as photographers, reporters or editors of newspapers, writers, police, fire persons, and city or county employees. Many of them are experts in their own right and can contribute information on such topics as: safety, burglar protection, photography, writing, and dealing with government.

Almost any topic a singles ministry may want as a program can be led by someone from within the community if it is of a moderate size. If a community is very small, leadership can be secured from within the county. Singles in very small communities, however, usually attend ministries in larger places.

In this discussion of outside leaders it is assumed that leaders come for a specific purpose and are limited to a short time. The group leader begins the meeting, introduces the program person, and later closes the meeting. The outside leader is not in total charge of the whole meeting but of a specific aspect: the program for that meeting.

Staff Person Leadership

"One of the things a leader has to watch out for is becoming the group. By that I mean he does all the planning, leading, and setting up the room. Just everything. It sounds crazy but a person who is ego-involved in getting a group going has a tendency to be all things to it."

This caution comes from a leader with these tendencies. The danger, here, is that the leader is so intent on the success of the group she or he fails to allow it to have a life of its own. This is not meant to discourage the development of programs by staff people. For most groups, having a person in charge of programs is most functional. However, planning programs and selecting resources should involve several participants. After all, the group members are adults with ideas, preferences, and needs.

The programs of two groups I contacted stand out. In one, the leader wrote the curriculum, an adult Bible study. In addition he developed a core of leaders and trained them for small group discussion. They, in turn, fed back to him the kinds of needs and feelings which were expressed during the table talks which were a major part of the meeting. He had spread the responsibility for the nurture of the group to about seventy other people who were selected and trained for their jobs.

This process worked well because the leader didn't try to do things he could not. For instance, a liaison with local counselors was set up so that singles in need of help could be sent to experts. Committees were established to handle the details of the group meetings. Other committees were organized to deal with the various interest and service activities of the group. The leader did what he could do—write the curriculum and train leaders. The leaders, in turn, provided him with continual feedback and new ideas.

On a smaller and more intimate scale, this is the manner in which several singles church school classes function. The leader is responsible for the curriculum and leads the group in its study/discussion while the group forms committees for other activities. The leader has a specific assignment and tries to keep to that. This doesn't limit him or her from participating in activities or being a colleague and friend. In terms of group tasks, however, the leader has a specific assignment.

An ingredient of this leadership style is giving people opportunities to put new ideas into the hopper. In order to be more helpful, some church school classes focus on issues rather than dwell on Bible study all the time. The issues are raised during discussions and catalogued for future classes. In such a setting the leader has a backlog of topics on which research may be done or resources collected. The pressure on the leader is that of having not a dearth but an overload of ideas.

Leaders who are faced with a limited amount of time and many topics may invite class members to help out. Class members who have become interested in a particular topic are invited to collect resources and do background work for the leader. While the individual may not want to lead the group, she or he does much work for the leader. This process is beneficial to the leader, the volunteer, and the group. In most such situations, the leader gives the volunteer a list of guidelines for searching out and noting the findings.

The other form of leader-developed program is based on a particular topic such as "Single Again" or "Children of Single-Again." As one leader explained, "We developed our own curricula because nothing seemed right for our group. Now I'm using it in several places because others seem to need it also."

This type of program is limited in duration and quite specific in content. It deals with a particular need and attracts only those with the need. It generally is narrow in focus and, because of this, not acceptable for larger groups. Its aim is not to expand a group so much as to allow people in the group to participate for a particular set of experiences.

For example, "Singles Again" as developed by one leader is an eight-session program. It is for those who have just been divorced and helps them to move into a regular singles group or to drop out following the eight weeks. The program is not a sustained program for a group but is limited to a homogeneous clientele for a brief period.

These types of packaged programs are rather common. The leaders take the packages from group to group or make them available to interested groups. In general this type of program is helpful *as an addition* to normal programming, but it should not be expected to be the regular fare for a heterogeneous group.

A Revolving Planning Committee

The revolving planning committee, one which regularly changes its personnel, is a convenient way to develop programs while including and training new leaders. This type of arrangement, where the tenure process assures that two-thirds of the committee are experienced and one-third are new recruits (see discussion following), permits a flow-through of people and ideas while keeping some continuity.

Suppose a singles ministry decides to begin a revolving planning committee. How does it go about it? Leaders decide on the number of members who will make up the committee; the number should be divisible by three. A revolving plan calls for a third of the committee membership to leave office after a set period of time. An example will show this process most clearly.

Six persons are chosen for the committee—persons A, B, C, D, E, and F. The rotation period is set at three months; every three months two persons go off the committee and two new persons come on. The members' terms, when the committee has rotated several times, are nine months in length. However, at the beginning of the committee's existence there are two "short" terms. The selection of who serves these is done by lot (see chart on next page).

The advantage of this system is that new people are working with experienced individuals. Both have an opportunity to learn from the other while neither is burdened with planning committee membership for a great length of time.

The primary assumption underlying the revolving planning committee

Time Period	Committee Membership
January–March	A, B, C, D, E, and F
April–June	C, D, E, F, G, and H
July–September	E, F, G, H, I, and J
October–December	G, H, I, J, K, and L

Persons A and B have served three months; C and D, six months; E and F, and all future committee members, will serve nine-month terms. The committee membership, though, will change in part every three months.

is that singles want to be involved but desire to limit their commitment of time and energy. (This is not a characteristic unique to singles.) They are willing to assist the group by giving time for a relatively short period but do not want long-term obligations.

A second assumption is that changing personnel will give a new perspective to the work of the committee. New people can contribute ideas which improve programs or lead to different types of programs. In addition, new people may have contacts which can tap previously unknown program resources.

One problem with this assumption is that a new perspective does not necessarily mean more creativity. One tendency of new committee members is to ''re-invent the wheel.'' That's the reason experienced people are the majority on the committee. Choosing the new personnel must be done carefully to encourage creativity.

Five reasons may make the revolving planning committee an attractive option for some ministries.

1. Singles have only limited time to invest in the group.

2. Singles are quite mobile.

3. Singles want to keep their long-term commitments to a minimum.

4. The involvement of many people in the organizational life of a group is a positive factor.

5. New people added to the planning committee help to keep the approach to programming fresh.

However, in all of the revolving and change, the planning committee must remain a miniature composite of the total group. This underscores the importance of the planning committee. Its composition is a key to developing and resourcing attractive programs for the target audience. If the committee is representative of the members of the ministry, it will sponsor programs which are interesting to the participants. If it isn't representative, the group will tend to change to become like the planning committee—or perhaps die out.

Evaluation

An important aim of this book is to provide information and guidance for leaders who are evaluating their ministry. It is essential for every ministry to evaluate its purpose regularly. Evaluation must underlie the concepts of redirection, program development, target identification, planning, and the other topics I have discussed. Even so, it is helpful to note briefly what formal evaluation accomplishes.

With regular evaluation you can accomplish the following: (1) identify past program topics which were helpful and might be repeated; (2) spot leaders or potential leaders who can lead future programs; (3) note problems in group organization and mechanics; and (4) ascertain whether the relationships with the congregation, pastor, and church leaders are being maintained.

1. *Identify repeatable program topics.* Most program leaders discover the need to explore issues from several perspectives. Any given program topic may excite interest when viewed from one angle but be totally boring from another. For example, the topic of "Managing Change" has been used in the adult program of our congregation annually for the past three years. Each time it has been developed from a different perspective and has met the needs of a different group of adults. Without evaluation, this topic would have been relegated to the "used" category and would not have been redesigned.

2. *Spot leaders.* Every ministry has people who can become good leaders on specific topics. They are the ones who can discuss a topic intelligently and who can bring new data to bear on issues. Without evaluation these people go unnoticed because the planning group doesn't compare notes about participants. In each group wishing to involve more of its own people, this part of evaluation is very important.

3. *Note operational and organizational problems.* No matter how smoothly a group runs, it still has the irritations and disjunctures which periodically afflict human groups. These may be caused by lack of communication, assumptions which are not tested, a little laziness, or any other of the normal negative aspects of humanity. In the rather closed arena of an evaluation session, questions can be raised, assumptions tested, and blame pinpointed. This can lead to fixing up the

operations and organization before the minor irritations become big problems. It is not wise to allow small things which can be remedied easily to cause crises.

4. *Revise relationships.* A great deal is at stake in any ministry. It is important to make sure people are kept informed and on board. An evaluation session can note the pastor's unease with some things about a ministry or a congregation's questioning about activities. In the small evaluation group, relationships essential to the continuance of the ministry can be reviewed and strategies developed to revise those needing repair.

The time span between evaluation meetings depends on the group but once a quarter is not too often for a group with more than fifty persons and once every six months is sufficient for smaller ministries.

The evaluators—the planning committee, pastor, and staff or volunteer leader—meet to look closely at each of the four items noted above for the time period (quarter or half year) under consideration. The meeting's purpose is to determine if the programs and group progress have met the aims set for the ministry at the beginning of the year. If there are problems, solutions are figured out and persons appointed to take care of them.

At least annually, during the planning session for the next year, the quarterly or half-year evaluations are reviewed to get a larger picture of the year. Their findings become an important part of the data on which the new year's programs are built.

Evaluation is usually done as a small-group discussion with someone taking notes. More formal evaluations, including the use of structured forms, need to be planned in advance and to involve the participants of the ministry. These kinds of evaluations usually occur every two or three years and are designed to test directions and processes. The most effective of these are done with the aid of persons not involved in the ministry.

6
Factors Which Affect
a Singles Ministry

No ministry exists in a vacuum. It is a living organism which is influenced by internal and external factors. Group size is an internal factor since it affects the interaction, programming, and leadership style of the ministry. It determines what is possible in terms of program and ministry development.

The key external factors affecting a group are location, building appearance, and competing ministries. When these are considered as having an effect on a ministry, the planning process is more intentional and can help the group cope more effectively. We will examine each of these more carefully.

Group Size

"The thing I like about our group is it's small. It's a size where we can relate well to each other. I have friends who can deal with me on caring terms."

"We are a large group and I think that attracts people. We have a lot to offer including special interest groups, all sorts of activities, socials, and volunteer projects. It's a madhouse around here all the time. I love it!''

"Our group is large but like all big groups it breaks down into smaller units. People get together because they like each other and have the same interests. Our aim is to provide plenty of opportunities for large and small group experiences.''

The size of a singles group is important for the following two reasons: (1) group size determines the range of possible activities; and (2) group size determines growth, stability, or stagnation. Size, as measured by numbers, tells what is possible in terms of programs and is one indicator of the health of a ministry. *Size is not the only evaluative indicator of a ministry,* but it is an important one.

The average attendance of a ministry is like the blood pressure of an individual. Combined with other indicators, it gives signals about the group. For instance, it suggests how extensive a range of activities the ministry can support. A group with an average attendance of six to ten will not be able to break into interest clusters, will not be large enough to divide into age or "type of singles" subunits, and cannot expect to have a much larger attendance at its programs. This doesn't mean the group is weak, just that it is limited in certain ways.

The other side of these limitations is the intimacy with which the small group members can deal with each other. They can develop strong support systems for everyone in the group. The group can become a social entity which is easy to manage.

Large groups find it expedient if not necessary to divide into smaller clusters. These give participants plenty of opportunity in which to receive personal attention and have interaction with others. In this way the benefits of a small group, intimacy and personal support, are created for members of large groups.

A large group which does not have small group traits is not attractive to singles for very long. Singles are searching for personal interaction and support, both of which come best through small groups. The burden of finding a level of size which gives the participants a feeling of intimacy as well as a feeling of belonging to a worthwhile venture falls on the planning committee. It must find the road to happiness between being too small and too large.

At the same time, the definitions of size are elastic and depend on the nature of the ministry and its constituency. There is no magic number which a group can use as the golden mean linking the closeness of a small group and the feeling of strength which comes from being a large group.

Even though the distinction between large and small is helpful in describing a ministry's characteristics and needs, number is not the only consideration. The popular psychology is to believe a successful singles ministry is one which is large, growing, and expanding in scope. Yet a ministry may be these, i.e., large, growing, expanding, and still not be effective in meeting its purposes. The quality of the program is more important than numbers. Many ministries accept this principle in theory but continue to evalute their effectiveness on the basis of how many come to each meeting. This is done without a view to whether or not singles are close by, other groups exist in nearby churches, or the ministry's own program meets the standards set for it.

There is more to a ministry than large numbers. Listen to one leader tell about the effects of growth on his group. "We're at the stage where we aren't sure we want to grow any larger. It has taken us quite awhile to get a group feel but we have it now. We are comfortable with each other and we can be very supportive. We also are hard on each other when the occasion demands. Our dilemma is whether we want to lose what we have gained by trying to get a bunch of new people in. We are undecided."

He went on to talk about the possibility of the group becoming exclusive and not giving visitors a feeling of being welcome. He spoke also of the dangers the group faced of becoming a crutch for its members rather than being supportive. It was a difficult choice facing the group, but the numbers game was not the only consideration for this leader.

Every group has a size at which it can function effectively. This is its optimum level. The boundaries around this level are built in at the beginning of the ministry. Group size is a product of the ministry's purpose, meeting time and place, leadership, and potential for attracting others. If the purpose or any other of these factors change, so does the size boundary. For example, a church school class is generally designed for no more than thirty attenders. Its meeting time, room size, and leadership style all affect the group's size. On the other hand, a group meeting in a large multi-room facility on a Sunday evening can attract many people without being crowded. If the meeting is a meal with a short program, the potential number of participants increases, and so must the facility size. The facility, which is chosen as a reflection of the group's purpose, puts the limits on the group's size.

It is when the group's size begins to exceed the room's capacity or when a group is so small as to be lost in a room that problems arise. A leader, describing the church school class which was the basis of his ministry, said, "We're as big as we can get. No more people would fit into the room even if we tried. We must either find a new room or start another class." His problem was rooted in the ministry's purpose (church school class experience), the size of the room (twenty-two-person capacity), the leadership style (popular to singles), and potential number of singles in the area (very large number).

Most groups level off to a comfortable operating size within a few months. The program, leadership, facility attractiveness, and size have coalesced to set some size boundaries. An average number of people can be predicted for each meeting. Once this happens, it takes a change in the nature and purpose of the group, new or different facilities, or a revamped program to create a new size. If a group decides it wants to change so as to increase its membership, some of the longtime members may be lost because they will not feel comfortable in a different sized group.

"How does a ministry, if its facilities and leader more or less determine its size, measure success?" Let's change the word "success" to effectiveness since this is the real measure of a ministry. Our question now is, "What influence does size have on the effectiveness of a ministry?"

The leader of a singles ministry independent of a congregation zeroes in on an answer to this question. "We try, through our program, to create an atmosphere in which all who come can be part of a small group. That's the format we use to help them minister to each other. We call these small groups 'clusters.' Getting new people involved in the clusters is the hardest test we face. The clusters do their work because of their leaders. I choose the cluster leaders carefully. They have been part of the ministry for some time and agree to work under my direction at this task. I train them to be cluster leaders for groups of six to ten other people. I meet with the cluster leaders each week to plan the activities for the total group. Our weekly meetings are the time when these leaders let me know about the need of any member for more help in the way of counseling. It works for us." This ministry has four-hundred members at its regular meetings.

The effectiveness of this ministry lies in its ability to link each member to someone who cares. It also gives the participants opportunities to work with or be counseled by the primary leader (who happens to be a trained and skilled counselor). It tries to give each participant, from the first visit, a simple procedure for becoming acquainted with others and involved in an intimate group. The emphasis is upon caring. At the same time, the atmosphere is one of a large group since the regular meetings include several hundred people. The effectiveness of the ministry rests on the abilities of the cluster group leaders to fulfill the purposes of the larger ministry. Note that nothing is left to chance; the leader trains and meets weekly with the cluster leaders.

This same idea, though the mechanics may vary because of the style of the leader, is used in many larger ministries. Each of the ministries, independent of the other, has discovered that the most effective way to meet the needs of singles is through smaller sharing-and-supporting clusters of others. The ministries are designed so people can move from one cluster to another in which they feel more comfortable. The ministries are organized carefully and leaders of the subunits are trained. However, there is no feeling of regimentation within any of these ministries.

Most tension regarding size is felt by groups which are at the "break point." This is the point at which growth is going to fracture the group into smaller units. When growth is steady, i.e., more people attend each meeting, pressure for change is more acutely felt by the members than if the group began large. Some of the regular members may feel as though something is being taken from them since they have to share their group with an ever-increasing number of others. The feeling will get so intense for some that they will need to leave the group and find another smaller one within which they can feel comfortable.

The size problem will not be solved without a decision by the leaders and members about their purpose as a singles ministry. No matter which direction is chosen, some people will be lost. If growth is chosen, a few will be disaffected. New people will be excluded if the intimacy of the original group is chosen.

If a group begins large or has grown large, the issue is to design opportunities for small group experiences. Intimacy can be possible in a large group but it takes effort and organization.

Location

The meeting facilities themselves limit the size of the group; their location sets boundaries on who will come as well. The location of a ministry is an important consideration of the potential of the group. Remember the mini-list of singles made for one congregation (chapter 1)? The singles were within two or three blocks of the church building. The apartment houses in which they lived had about fifty other singles, a percentage of whom could be considered potential members. The location of the congregation would make a ministry possible.

Two considerations are important when selecting a location for a ministry. The first is the living places of the members and the second is where they work. One ministry cited previously met downtown between 5 and 6 P.M. in order to accommodate people who worked downtown. The premise of the location and time was that potential participants would not return downtown for a meeting once they had left. It was also viewed as a metropolitan ministry so the location had to be in a central place. The final selection of site was made because of its accessibility to potential participants.

The most effective ministries are in places which are easily found by potential participants. Large groups do not meet in an out-of-the-way small neighborhood church. Members would have trouble finding it and it would not have parking facilities for large numbers. For these reasons the meeting places for large ministries are in churches which are known throughout the area, are visible from major streets, and require few directions to find. People do not want to be frustrated in searching out a ministry.

On the other hand, ministries catering to members of a congregation or focusing on the singles in a particular neighborhood, usually through a church school class, will have few problems in attracting their group because of location. Since the church is known and the people are familiar with it, location is not an issue unless the ministry tries to change its purpose.

The target population and purpose make a difference in both the place and the schedule of the programs. Thus, groups which are for residents of suburban areas will find a church which is well-known and set their meeting times no earlier than 8 P.M. The reason is that members must commute to the meeting. People need time to get home from work, eat, do whatever chores or errands they must, and then drive on to the meeting. This means the church has to be in a convenient location and the meeting time must be reasonable.

The key to time scheduling, as well as selecting a site, is knowing the group. If possible, the participants can help set the time for meetings but the availability of the facilities may limit the possibilities. If the times which are open at a building are not in the best interests of a group, a new place ought to be found.

A combination of location, meeting time, and type of meeting attracts people to a ministry. Keeping this in mind, set the meeting time to allow commuters to relax after work before coming out to a meeting. Also pick a spot for the meeting that is easy to get to even for a stranger in the area.

Building Appearance

Anyone who has been responsible for meetings knows the effect a building has on a group. No matter how good the planned program is, if the room is not attractive, the feeling of the group will be somewhat negative. On the other hand, if a room is cheerful and exudes warmth, even a mediocre program can result in a good feeling within the group. The setting of the program, the room, will enliven or dampen the spirits of those who come.

Each ministry must assess its meeting place and rate the positive and negative features. If the total rating leans toward the negative, it is a good idea either not to meet there or to do something about the room to make it more acceptable. It makes little sense to go to a lot of work planning a program and have it fail because of the room.

What is a group looking for as it rates a room? If the building has an odor of any kind—for instance, some churches smell musty—its attractiveness is questionable for many people: They can't stand the particular odor or it makes their allergies act up or something else. That first smell can turn people off to a group without their even participating in a program.

What condition the meeting place is in is another factor in bringing people back. Rooms in disrepair, broken furniture, fixtures that don't work, and unusable toilets are things which visitors do not feel they have to tolerate. Neither is a room acceptable if it has no air circulation or is extremely warm or quite cold. Most of these items are correctable and should be attended to before a group begins to meet in a place. It is up to the planning committee to judge the room's acceptability.

If all of the above conditions are met satisfactorily yet when the singles arrive the doors are locked, no lights are on, the halls are cluttered, and the parking area has no space, there is still a problem. While these are not in the room itself, they impinge on people as they attempt to get to the room. Such items are important for the committee to consider as well.

While these comments assume most ministries will meet in a church, this is not always the case. Some meet in an annex or parish house, in parsonages, in private homes, and in public meeting rooms. It is still the responsibility of the planning committee to make certain these places create the kind of atmosphere desired for the group. After all, the place of meeting is an expression of the purpose of the ministry.

Using the church is an asset to most groups because they have a room for themselves. When a group doesn't have regular access to a room or rooms because other organizations of the congregation take precedence in space usage, the singles ministry will quickly fold or find other quarters. This doesn't mean special activities of the church need to be cancelled because the singles want to meet that particular night. It means a schedule is agreed on and the singles ministry is given the same consideration as every other group which meets regularly. The singles ministry ought not be a second-rate organization.

It is likewise true that singles groups should be bound by the same rules and regulations observed by other organizations. In fact, no singles ministry which I contacted had any privileges or obligations other organizations did not have. The singles ministry was one of the groups sponsored by the church and was expected to live within the limits of sponsorship spelled out at the beginning of the ministry.

How do singles feel about meeting in the church?

"The church doesn't make any difference to our group. They rather like the idea as long as they are not required to attend church services. If that happened, we would lose many of our members but I don't see that happening. The congregation is pretty much behind us."

This leader's statement is a summary of many others. They want their groups to meet in the church because of the atmosphere a church meeting creates. It is a special feeling that separates it from groups meeting in secular places. Groups considering another type of place to hold meetings should think carefully about the image of a church building and its effect on a group.

A few ministries occasionally meet in members' homes. These groups usually have fewer than a dozen members and use this as a treat for a dinner or celebration of some sort. They normally use the church building and the home meeting is a change of pace.

Other ministries enhance their programs by meeting occasionally in a restaurant for a meal. This limits participation because of cost, accommodations, or reservations but it is an alternative to the regular meeting place. Other ministries try hard to have some of their activities outside the regular meeting place so participants do not feel the ministry is in a rut.

An issue for some singles is the type of activities not permitted in the church building. Drinking is not permitted in many churches and social dancing is not permissible in some. Few churches frown on square or folk dancing. However, drinking and social dancing are attractive to many singles and several leaders said one tension in the group's use of the church centered on these prohibitions. They went on to say these tensions were healthy and did not limit the group's activities even though dancing and drinking were not allowed.

Competitive Ministries

In larger communities and cities, the singles ministry in a congregation is not likely to be the only game in town. There will be alternatives in the form of another ministries. Such competition is not unknown for church leaders. They are accustomed to seeing other groups in the community providing the same types of services.

One of the steps at the beginning of a ministry and at each evaluation point is gathering information about the other ministries. This information makes it possible for a congregation and its ministry to focus on a group and a program style which is not being dealt with by the other ministries. It was on the basis of a year's work of looking and learning that one ministry decided on its unique contribution to singles through a ministry. In fact, many groups spend six to nine months in research before starting or redirecting their ministry.

In some instances it may be most economical and effective to sponsor joint programs. This happens in places where the ministries work ecumenically to provide special activities or programs which none of them individually can sponsor. This is using competition creatively since none of the singles groups curtails its programs.

7

Group Needs

Humans must have air to breathe, water to drink, and food to eat if they are to survive. Groups must have people, positive relationships, a set of symbols, a place to meet, and someone who is a leader in order to continue to exist. These are air, water, and food for groups.

Groups are not born; they must be built. Each singles ministry begins as a potential group. However, in most singles ministries, the members come and go with little apparent concern for maintaining the group's life. While this is a given in voluntary organizations which attract people on the basis of interest and perceived need, a group has to be molded in order for a ministry to be developed. It is the task of the sponsoring agency and the leadership to construct the mechanisms which ensure the group's continued existence.

The former list of needs have been the focus of this book. It is time to look at the forces surrounding the ministry—the environment. The attitude of the sponsoring group determines the environment: nurturing, hostile, apathetic, or laissez-faire. The last is often not considered to be an attitude, yet it *is* and it has an effect on the ministry. The environment can be of life-or-death importance for a singles ministry.

One leader told about his efforts to make certain the environment was supportive. He reported, "We took over a year to build the relationships and gain support within the congregation so the ministry wouldn't fold because of internal opposition. We met with the Board, the pastor, church leaders, and with the education people. We met not once but several times with each of them so they knew what we had in mind and how we wanted to move. We took each step with their knowledge and full support. This has meant so much as we have encountered the normal problems of interpretation and use of facilities. We just go back to our leaders and remind them of their commitments. It has meant a really stressless time for us."

This external environment, during the embryonic months of a ministry, is the most essential aspect of group life. It is this environment which will provide leaders, training, finances, and support as the group tries to build itself. These are the needs of the group which a congregation provides.

It is this foundation supplied by the congregation which will allow a singles ministry to succeed or fail. What is needed from a congregation? Pastoral commitment and support, congregational support, and adequate leadership recruitment and training are the basics. Not one of these is expendable. If one is missing, the ministry will not have the substance to last through even a minor crisis. It is important to look at each one of these in more detail.

Pastoral Support

The pastor is the lifeline of any group to the official church body. She or he is the one to whom the congregation looks for interpretation and opinion on any issue facing it. On her or his shoulders rests the burden of deciding how far a congregation can go in supporting a group affiliated with the church. A word from the minister will head off problems before they can become issues.

In congregations with a staff, most issues can be solved in conversation with the staff person responsible for a group. In a singles ministry, this is usually an assistant or associate minister assigned as liaison who works closely with the group's leaders. Since the associate is close to the group, he or she will be able to interpret its needs and wishes to the senior pastor and to the Board. However, all of the associates whom I contacted felt it was necessary to have the senior pastor linked closely to the singles. Otherwise, when a problem arose, the associate (with less credibility and power than the senior pastor) might be unable to explain and defend adequately the singles to the Board.

The importance of the pastor should not be underestimated. In the following quotations, her or his role is explained by various leaders. The word minister or pastor in these quotations refers to the person who is directly linked to the singles ministry. This may be an associate, an assistant, or a director of education.

"The minister was instrumental in getting the group started. He helped in our planning sessions for the first few months and comes now and then to our programs. He's always welcome and he shows his interest but he doesn't have to be here at all. He just wants to keep our ties strong."

"The senior pastor has been a lifesaver several times. He has helped with recruiting and training some of our leaders. He has explained the program to the Board when the question of the types of people who come was raised. He stepped in to find resource people for us a few times. We feel like when we have a need, he is there to help."

"I wouldn't take a step without the minister being behind me. It's true that my assignment is single adult ministry but my 'legitimation' rests in the hands of the senior minister. Only he will be heard when the crunch comes. That's the reason I let him know what's going on and how things seem to be shaping up. It's smart politics from my perspective."

"We'd be lost without the minister. He encouraged us to get started, asked the secretary to help us with setting up the list of singles in the church, talked to us about the need for establishing peripheral services like counseling, worked with us in determining facility needs and getting the clearance for that, and pushes us for regular reports to the Board. He has been our behind-the-scenes stimulant and planner."

The minister is important! She or he is not needed once or twice but *throughout* the life of the group. The environment over which the group has no control must be monitored by a sympathetic person who can influence both the group and the environment. This person is the pastor.

The preceding quotations suggest a chronology for a minister's involvement in a singles ministry. The critical points appear to be: identifying need, working with the original planning committee, considering the range of programs, helping with publicity, being at the initial meeting, and maintaining continual contact. Let's look at each of these.

1. *Need Identification.* A key role for ministers is that of being aware of the need for a singles ministry. This happens in one of two ways: (1) the minister is or becomes single, or (2) some people in the church or community suggest to the minister a need for a singles ministry. In either case, the minister begins looking at the congregation in a new light. He or she "puts on new glasses" to search out singles and possibilities for singles programs in the life of the congregation.

A few pastors I contacted said, "I didn't know anything about singles ministry. I was too busy and I felt someone else could do it better. But they [singles] wouldn't listen. They kept up the pressure and you can see the result. I had to help!" As these pastors talked further it was obvious they were not as reluctant as their first impression suggested. They became convinced the congregation had to include this important and neglected group. They pushed hard once they understood the need.

2. *Planning Group Participation.* After discovering a need and doing research, the minister typically calls together a small group of singles to act as a planning committee. These people usually work together for several months to develop the purpose, refine the research in order to target a group, and execute the plans which eventuate in a meeting. The planning group varies in size from three to six and includes those who raised the issue of a singles ministry in the first place.

The first task of this team is to review the list of singles compiled by the pastor or the church secretary or to make one. In this run-through, the singles may add to the list such designations as age, type of singleness, length of singleness, possibilities of interest in a ministry, and skills the individual might bring to the group. This phase completed, the group, with the minister's leading, turns to program considerations.

3. *Program Planning.* Resource materials from the denomination, experiences of other congregations, and conversations with other clergy give the minister materials regarding programs to bring to the planning group. It is because of this information that the pastor can assist the planning group to think about program possibilities in this congregation.

The minister is particularly helpful here because decisions about programs focus on target populations. In discussing program possibilities, the planning group must seriously consider who can be reached with what and how. The minister needs to help keep realism in the planning group so that frustration does not immobilize future efforts.

4. *Publicity*. The minister, with access to the normal church publicity channels, can help the group plan to use publicity most effectively. Church secretaries, because of their workload, are reluctant to assume any additional tasks, especially publicity for a new group. In most churches, singles do their own newsletters, bulletins, and the like. They also take care of the news releases and stories in local papers.

The singles need to have a time set aside at the church office when they can do their publicity work. This time ought to be scheduled for their benefit at the same time care is being taken not to interfere with normal office routine. The minister can help relieve this bottleneck by setting priorities in the office and in the group so that the use of equipment will not lead to conflict. The minister's role is to help the singles and the secretary create operational guidelines.

5. *Initial meeting*. The minister probably will be present at the initial meeting but will not lead it. The functions he or she performs will be to mix with the singles, participate as they do in the program, and be introduced so he or she can announce other parts of the church's program which might be of interest to singles. This low profile will not be used by ministers who are the leaders of singles groups. It is the normal approach of senior ministers, associates, other staff, or volunteers who have been assigned responsibility for liaison with the singles ministry. These people need to be viewed as backup, support-type leaders.

6. *Continuing Contact*. The last and continuing step in the minister's relationship to the singles group is that of keeping communication lines open with the leaders. This may be on a "whenever-I-can-make-it" basis or on a particular meeting schedule. It most likely will be the "whenever-I-can-make-it" motif since this works the best and is satisfactory for most singles ministries. No matter what the arrangement is for contact, the minister must honor the agreement to be effective with the group.

This process relationship is not the only role of the minister in a singles ministry. He or she is the link with the official church body. Reports, analyses, recommendations, and critiques relating to the ministry should be heard and reviewed by the minister. It is assumed the minister is sympathetic since one opposed to the group would see to its extinction in short order.

It is important for the congregation's governing body to have regular information about the group and its activities. While most groups do not depend on this body for their existence, the Board does control the facilities and can help in many ways such as giving money, helping to find resource persons, and assisting in leadership recruitment. The minister is the vital link which conveys the needs of the group to the Board and encourages their interactions.

Congregational Support

"Most of the congregation doesn't know anything about our program. They are interested in all the church's programs but are most involved only in those which directly affect them. Having said that, they have not been critical or raised questions about what we do. I feel they are supportive."

"We have never asked the congregation for anything they have not agreed to do or to give. They support us out of the regular budget and by providing facilities and janitorial services. Once in a while the pastor will pass on a comment or question he has picked up on visiting. A few of them are critical but most are curious about who we are and what we do."

"Our program is like a scout troop at the church. We are affiliated but have a separate existence. The church helped us get started by giving us some money and they pay the minister who works part time with singles. But as far as them impacting us or us impacting them, it doesn't happen."

These comments are descriptive of a neutral relationship which is a misleading perception of singles ministries; many ministries do feel they have a life and program independent of the church. But this is as much a myth as saying any organization of the church is not related to or supported by the congregation. Silence doesn't mean apathy nor does it convey little interest or concern. It generally means the congregation is not informed.

A congregation with a singles ministry either supports it or doesn't support it. There is no such thing as letting a ministry live on its own. While the involvement of the congregation may be quiet, there are several ways in which the congregation has an impact on a ministry. Let's look at a few of them.

1. *Facilities*. A congregation provides the meeting place for many

single adult ministries. As with any organization of the church, this is done on a conditional basis. The conditions for continued use are: Each group must treat the building with respect; certain kinds of activities are not allowed; certain rooms have particular uses (such as the sanctuary); and the group is reponsible for closing the doors, turning off the heat and lights, and leaving the facilities reasonably clean. This means if something is broken, walls are defaced, rest rooms are left in deplorable condition, smoking occurs in nonsmoking areas, lights are left on after the meeting, or whatever, the group's leader will need to give the reasons for these problems to the pastor and the group will need to fix up, clean up, or pay for the fixing.

The facilities are provided usually without charge even though many of the participants of the ministry may not be members of the congregation. The fact that facilities are free saves the ministry quite a lot of money each year. The ministry needs to remember this with a note of appreciation to the appropriate church board or committee at least once a year.

2. *Minister's time.* A congregation usually underwrites the cost of giving pastoral leadership to the ministry. The congregation may ask or allow the minister to take time to help a group organize, assist it in planning, serve as a resource person, and give counseling to participants. While this seems normal to a ministry, let's remember the words of leaders, ''Most of these people aren't members here and will never become our members. We are providing a service to them in the name of the church.''

Everything costs. A minister giving time to a single adult ministry takes it from other activities. Most congregations don't look for a return on everything it sponsors but the minister's time is accountable. The minister is to serve the congregation's members first and when it becomes obvious that most of his or her counseling time is taken up by single adults who are not related to the church, members can legitimately question this time usage. The congregation can ask if the singles would be equally served by going to a counselor on a pay-as-you-go basis. This appears to be a rather common problem in larger ministries.

This in no way suggests a minister's services should be limited only to the congregation. That is self-defeating and out of character for a Christian group. The point to be understood by the singles ministry is that a professional staff member or a volunteer costs a congregation.

The time used with the singles ministry is taken from other equally worthwhile ventures. Therefore, it is smart to keep the working relationship between the singles and the congregation in harmony. This requires continuous communication and a recognition by each of the legitimacy of the ministry performed by the other.

3. *Financial Support.* Most singles ministries receive some direct financial support from the congregation. This is in addition to the free use of facilities, assistance with publicity, duplicating work done in the office, and professional guidance from the minister or an associate. The amount of direct aid is usually relatively small but does help to defray costs for speakers, to purchase supplies, to get printing done, or to help with expenses the group would otherwise find impossible to meet. This cash outlay is supplemental to the money raised and used by the singles ministry itself. It is an extra evidence of concern by the congregation.

The list of ways congregations support a ministry could be extended but the ways mentioned are enough to refute the idea that a congregation's silence means lack of interest, concern, and support. No matter how concern is expressed—through a building, a staff person responsible for the singles ministry, or money—the congregation has a stake in the group. Because of this, the congregation should be given opportunities to hear about what the group is doing, what it needs, and in what ways the church members can help the singles group. At the same time, the singles ministry ought to expect critical input from the congregation the same as every other organization receives critical analysis. Some tension is needed to prevent even a harmonious relationship from growing stale and stagnating.

One leader of an effective singles ministry elaborated on congregational support as he said, "Anytime we need something, the congregation is there to offer help. They don't often give us money but they give us experience, guidance, attendance at special events and fundraisers, and are just open to us. They treat us like people. That's what we like so much about the church. They make us feel like we are people worth listening to and working with."

Openness is an important attribute for sponsors of singles ministries. Yet it is very hard to achieve. Openness seems to be especially difficult for congregations with ministries which attract mostly divorced persons. A congregation, most of whose members consider divorce to be unnecessary and highly undesirable, will tend to have a biased view of divorced singles. The congregation will feel threatened and will have a hard time thinking of these singles as "our kind of people." Yet, openness is a part of becoming Christian and should be the goal of each congregation.

It is helpful to remember the meaning of openness. It is not an acceptance of all a person or group stands for or does. Webster's Seventh New Collegiate Dictionary defines "open" as: "characterized by ready accessibility and a cooperative attitude which is . . . willing to hear and consider or to accept and deal with."

A congregation with an open attitude toward its singles ministry is one in which the official governing body, the pastor, and the church members are cooperative and accessible. They do not isolate the singles ministry even though they may not appreciate everything about the singles' pattern or philosophy. The church members are willing to help the singles ministry in whatever ways they can that do not violate their own beliefs and life patterns. This attitude is one of respect.

A major factor affecting the relationship between the congregation and the singles ministry is how communication takes place between them. Publicity about singles programs and church programs, getting singles involved in the church activities outside their own group, and regular reports to the Board are the most common methods for maintaining mutual understanding. Of these three methods the most helpful appears to be getting singles involved in other aspects of the church's program. This type of encounter provides growth not only for the single but for the groups with whom she or he interacts in the life of the congregation.

Leadership Recruitment and Training

"Our group rotates all of its positions during the year. It takes a lot of work at recruiting [to fill the positions] but it keeps the interest high and assures us of strong programming. We let the people know when they first come we would like them to participate on one of the committees. It's never 100 percent but I think we get over half of our people to really participate in the organizational part of the group."

"The minister helps us with the training. We spend time each year training people to do the various jobs associated with their offices like running a meeting, doing publicity (including how to mimeograph things), setting up for programs, learning where equipment is kept and how to operate it. There is a whole raft of things like that we go over with new people at least once a year. It takes time but it certainly makes for a smoother operation.''

Two fundamentals in group life are recruitment and training of leaders. These take time and continuous effort. Given the characteristics of singles and singles ministries, it should come as no surprise to hear that the most effective ministries have an unceasing leader-recruitment policy. "We are always on the lookout for good leaders and people who want to get involved" is an operational philosophy for most groups.

However, it is one thing to be on the lookout for leaders and quite a different process to recruit effectively and utilize their skills. Targeting is the most efficient way to go about recruiting. In the same way that the group identifies its potential participants, it should focus on the kinds of leaders it needs. List the jobs, identify traits of the person who would do each job well, and then go look for the people.

The ministries which reverse this procedure, i.e., find a person and then tailor the job to fit him or her, end up serving the needs of the person rather than benefiting the group. This is a good way to get people involved but involvement must help build the group if the ministry is to be effective.

The most important part of recruiting is having firmly in mind a description of the job needing to be done. This doesn't mean being wed to a particular process for accomplishing the task; it means being clear about what the job is and what results are expected. There are usually alternative ways of doing any task and people ought to be given some freedom in using their skills in fulfilling an assignment. However, the time schedule and the expected results ought to be plainly spelled out (explained verbally two or three times and then written down) so no one will suffer from weak instructions or can claim misdirection.

Personality preferences always enter into recruitment. We all like certain kinds of people more than others and we tend to select the ones we like as leaders more often. This isn't sinful or even disruptive of the group. It does mean, however, that the group is being limited by not having more pluralism and leaders with diverse interests. Therefore, if a group wants to be efficient and select a cross section of people without reference to personality preferences, it will be more purposeful in its recruitment.

One method is to use a committee whose task it is to set up the jobs and criteria for people to fill them. The committee then takes the list of participants and selects persons to contact who might be able to do each task. A limited time schedule is given the committee so its work is done relatively quickly. This method takes recruitment out of the hands of an individual and reduces, though does not eliminate, bias.

An alternative approach is to use the interest finder survey (see chapter 3). Semiannually a brief survey form with a listing of jobs is circulated at one or two meetings. People are given a few minutes to complete it by noting which tasks they would be willing to do. These forms are collected and turned over to the recruitment committee.

It then becomes the responsibility of the recruitment committee to select and fit people to the jobs. Everyone who wants to be on a committee may not be capable or needed. The committee must make the necessary judgments. The selections ought to be made on as rational a basis as possible rather than on rumor or personal like or dislike. Persons' methods for doing a job may differ but as long as the job is well done, this may be all that is required. Of course, if a person is abrasive, not easy to get along with, unpredictable, or not dependable, the committee will not assign her or him to a position on which the group depends.

The selections don't always work out as expected. What happens then? First, someone should talk about the problem with the person causing the trouble. Then, if the person doesn't do the job, the appropriate leader can ask for a resignation. If this doesn't work, the actual responsibilities for the job may be assumed by someone else even though the ineffective individual has the title. A third method for dealing with this situation is to create a new job and title so someone can assume the duties of the person who will not resign. Any of these is a legitimate and useful way of getting a job done while not degrading or demoralizing a recalcitrant title holder. Of course, the manner in which the person is requested to make a change will often make a difference in the way he or she responds.

Recruitment is only the first step in getting leaders for a group. The second step is equally important: training the persons for the jobs and for work in this group. Most singles ministries have no formal training process other than "on-the-job experience." This places a tremendous burden on the new person who must learn duties and boundaries as she or he goes along. This has the advantage of allowing the newcomer a lot of leeway in style and method. On the other hand it frustrates her or him by not clearly identifying what has to be done, how, and when. On-the-job training is important, but that is the second half of the process. The first half of the training is ignored by most groups.

The forgotten half of training is the job description plus instruction in the ground rules for working at the church and/or with the secretary, the finances related to the task, and the names of people who will be working at the same time. These things could be discovered later on, but who needs embarrassing surprises that could be avoided? Certainly not adults who have little time to give to a group! It's better to spend some time at the beginning going over the details and providing written materials than to have an individual quit because of total frustration or because "everybody keeps changing the rules."

Training takes such a small amount of time that it should be standard procedure. Even if people have served as leaders or members of committees before, their information can be updated and their memory refreshed about policies and procedures. What a church office takes for granted, people who must deal with the office may know nothing about. Poor working relations because of ignorance have cost some groups the loss of some very good group leaders. These group leaders felt they didn't have to put up with the inefficiency or intransigency in the church's office. What they didn't know were the rules governing the office's work. The people in the office were just doing their job; they weren't being inefficient or obstinate.

Single adults are usually working people. They are accustomed to receiving training and instruction before assuming a task. When the singles ministry doesn't provide the same kind of consideration to a person in a job the ministry depends on for its existence, the volunteer begins to feel that the job is not all that important. A job has expected results, ways for doing it, and procedures for dealing with people. A working single knows this and expects to be told these particulars as he or she becomes a leader in the ministry.

The recruitment committee is responsible for training. It may enlist the aid of the minister and others in the church who can help. No matter who assists, the training occurs just before a person assumes office. A training session will take about a hour and a half. It will take people through their particular responsibilities, identify policies of the church which affect them, provide a tour of the church office to show where supplies and equipment are kept, and give an introduction to secretaries and volunteers who will be working with the leaders. Through training, persons can discover how the jobs were done previously and what can be expected in terms of cooperation, deadlines, supplies, and expenses.[1] This training time will then be supplemented by on-the-job experience.

The church staff (minister and custodian at the least) will need to know what persons in the group have which jobs. It's as important for the church staff to know the singles ministry leaders as it is for these incumbents to know the church staff. Thus, communication channels have to be rebuilt any time there is a change in officers. This need for communication is enough to justify regular training sessions.

Keeping It Going

The desire to have a group is the greatest reason for getting a singles ministry started. It isn't possible to develop a group without people who want to belong. Strong interest among potential participants determines the feasibility of starting and maintaining a ministry. If people want one badly enough to help get it started, they will be a long step down the road to setting up a ministry they will want to maintain.

But desire is only the beginning. It takes a lot of careful planning and hard work to translate the desire for a group into a functioning group. Selecting the right leaders, finding an adequate meeting place, developing interesting programs, setting a meeting time, and creating social and recreational activities which augment the programs are critical elements in a good ministry. None of these just happen. It takes effort, or as an ad says, "old-fashioned hard work."

One thing yet is needed, to paraphrase Jesus. A group with members who make only short-term commitments must design its organizational life to take advantage of this fact. Not many groups have developed a philosophy and operating style which allows them to use the skills and talents of their members in disconnected and short spans of time. It's hard to do since one of the factors of group life is the need for continuity of experience. Groups must find a way to bind the future, present, and past into a package which accomplishes group purpose and gives group members a sense of what the ministry is, what it has been, and what it will be.

[1] For a more detailed description of training for volunteers see chapter 6 of my book *The Care and Feeding of Volunteers* (Nashville: Abingdon Press, 1978).

The most effective way for assuring continuity is to have a staff person, a minister, or a volunteer who functions as the backup, the link, and the coordinator for the group. With such a person holding things together, a group can effectively use the short-term pieces of time and effort from the officers.

Large ministries, those with more than fifty in regular attendance at meetings, find they cannot do much without such a person. In some groups, this task is handled by a volunteer or a volunteer couple. In other groups, the church hires a part-time or full-time staff member just for the singles work. In still other congregations, the pastor assumes this work. The primary tasks of this individual are coordination, planning, and administrative details.

"Our group took off this year because we were able to hire a minister for singles. She brought together the organization and put everything on an operational basis. Before she came we were trying to piece things together by using many people all of whom could give just a smidgen of time."

"Our group is small because if it got any larger we couldn't handle it. We don't have the time to give to the organization. None of us has more than a little time we can give each week and that's barely enough to keep what program we have going."

"We had to drop our program because the minister dealing with singles left. He was responsible for everything and when he left no one was in a position to pick up the operations. The singles all depended on him and when they saw the tremendous amount of effort and time required to keep things going, they decided to drop it for awhile and start again in a few months."

One part of the effectiveness of the leaders in a singles ministry is the ability and commitment of the person who does the behind-the-scenes work to keep everything moving. In church school classes this is often the teacher. He or she is responsible for the lesson presentation and will preside during the discussions about additional and future activities. It will often be this individual's task to clear dates with the church and make mechanical arrangements, i.e., secure tickets, make reservations, and the like, for special events. Sometimes the teacher refuses to do these things and a volunteer from the class must act as the administrator.

Groups like to have their officers work closely with an adviser from the church. The adviser functions like a sponsor of a youth group. She or he takes part in the planning meetings, makes suggestions about procedures, and is the link with the church. Very often this person has a place on the Board to represent the singles ministry. This type of official relationship assures continuity within the ministry and regular feedback to the congregation.

The primary leader functions as the symbol of continuity with the other ministries in the church. This person must have had leadership experience and have been active in the church previously to function effectively in this capacity. Such a position takes time and requires a knowledge of the church and its resources. It isn't a job for a neophyte to the congregation.

Groups cannot function effectively without a person or core group that makes certain that programs happen, publicity gets out, and meetings are held. This drudge work is not rewarded with anything except the group's continuing existence. Those who perform these duties have assumed them so the ministry can survive.

It is essential for a congregation to consider the maintenance of the group before the ministry is started. Assuming that a ministry will maintain itself effectively will not make it do so. A ministry is much more likely to thrive if the Board or a minister undertakes the responsibility to find a person or small group that will perform the continuity tasks. The person or group will need to be good at details, tenacious in getting information and clearances, and very dependable.

This book provides a map for work with singles ministries based on the experiences of several of them. In its discussions it also points out the need for each ministry to be unique and for each church to develop its singles ministry according to the needs and desires of its people. As with other ministries, the human needs which can be met by a congregation are best done with an eye to "our people."

The emphasis is upon being intentional and planning carefully. A singles ministry can be threatening to other programs merely because it is different. Yet the need is great. The challenge has been presented; it is now up to the congregation to proceed.

Appendix

Selected Books

William V. Arnold, et al., *Divorce: Prevention or Survival*. Philadelphia: The Westminster Press, 1977.

Velma T. Carter and J. Lynn Leavenworth, *Putting the Pieces Together*. Valley Forge: Judson Press, 1977.

Nicholas B. Christoff, *Saturday Night, Sunday Morning*. New York: Harper & Row, Publishers, Inc., 1978.

William Lyon, *A Pew for One, Please*. New York: The Seabury Press, Inc., 1977.

Miriam B. Nye, *But I Never Thought He'd Die: Practical Help for Widows*. Philadelphia: The Westminster Press, 1978.

Gail Sheehy, *Passages*. New York: E. P. Dutton, 1976.

Denominational Offices

Most denominations have a person or persons responsible for ministry to single adults in their education office or division. A selected list of denominations is given. A more complete listing is in the *Yearbook of American and Canadian Churches,* 1981, editor Constant H. Jacquet, Jr., published annually in Nashville, Tennessee, by Abingdon Press.

American Baptist Churches in the U.S.A.
Board of Educational Ministries, Ministry with Adults
Valley Forge, PA 19481

Christian Church (Disciples of Christ)
Division of Homeland Ministries
222 S. Downey Avenue (Box 1986)
Indianapolis, IN 46206

Cumberland Presbyterian Church
Board of Christian Education
Box 40149 (1978 Union Avenue)
Memphis, TN 38104

Lutheran Church in America
Division for Parish Services
2900 Queen Lane
Philadelphia, PA 19129

Presbyterian Church in the United States
Division of National Missions
341 Ponce de Leon Avenue, NE
Atlanta, GA 30308

The Sunday School Board, SBC
Family Ministry Department
127 Ninth Avenue, North
Nashville, TN 37234

United Church of Christ
United Church Board for Homeland Ministries
132 West 31st Street
New York, NY 10001

United Methodist Church
Board of Discipleship

P. O. Box 840 (1908 Grand Avenue and 1001 19th Avenue, South)
Nashville, TN 37202

United Presbyterian Church in the USA
The Program Agency
475 Riverside Drive
New York, NY 10027